HOSPITALITY AND TOURISM MANAGEMENT STRATEGIES

HOSPITALITY AND TOURISM MANAGEMENT STRATEGIES

SUNIL SHARMA

AKANSHA PUBLISHING HOUSE
NEW DELHI

AKANSHA PUBLISHING HOUSE
R 37-B, Vani Vihar, Uttam Nagar
New Delhi-110059
Email: ektabooks@yahoo.com

Showroom
4649-B/21, Ansari Road
Daryaganj, New Delhi - 110 002
Phones: 011-23263193, 9811582579

Hospitality and Tourism Management Strategies

First Edition 2005
ISBN 81-8370-020-9

PRINTED IN INDIA

Published by M.P. Misra for Akansha Publishing House, New Delhi and
Printed at : Mehra Offset Press, New Delhi

Contents

Preface

The present volume is a valuable resource for those concerned with the tourism industry. The author has used his many years of experience as a tourism operator and a hotel manager to give a general guide for developing successful and sustainable tourism programmes within an economic market. This is not a 'how-to' book with clear, step-by-step instructions, but rather an analytical discussion of the methods, components, and techniques that characterise effective tourism management strategies.

The book looks at the impact tourism has on the economic, social, and cultural status of the travel destination. It also discuss the management objectives and developmental conditions, all derived from common pool resources management research done in the last fifty years. The factors and conditions that must be considered once the development plan has been created and put into effect are described in detail. Quality-, quantity-, and location-based growth management strategies are also examined, along with the role of the market, local norms, plus the hierarchical scales often encountered in the implementation of these strategies.

The book insists that the local community, tourists, and state/national governments all share in the responsibility and accountability for the development, management and success of any tourism and hospitality development programme, and a balanced effort and equitable involvement are the key ingredients for its planning. The reader is reminded that local geographic, cultural, and societal characteristics play significant roles in determining which strategy should be employed for a specific region. Numerous case studies from around the world are included to highlight concepts and points brought up in the discussion.

This book will be a highly useful reference tool for and students, teachers are professionals in the field of tourism and hospitality management. It will also be useful for politicians, government officials, community leaders, and others directly involved in tourism development planning.

Editor

1

Dimensions of Sustainable Development

Travel and tourism is now one of the largest industries in the world. Economically, it creates jobs and contributes over 10% Gross Domestic Product (GDP), as well as brings in capital investment and exports. Socially and culturally, travel and tourism offers the opportunity of providing jobs for minority and disadvantaged groups, creating adequate training in management skills, education and technology to local people and increasing incomes in rural and local economies, thereby contributing to the alleviation of poverty in developing countries.

In 1992 at the Rio Earth Summit, 178 governments approved Agenda 21 and the Rio Declaration. Agenda 21 offered a blueprint for sustainable development, while the Rio Declaration articulated the main principles for sustainable development in the 21st century. Both documents challenged organisations, governments and industries to work towards maximum levels of sustainability, defined by the Brundtland Commission in 1987 as 'development that meets the needs of the present without compromising the ability of future generations to meet their own needs'.Since the summit, the social, political and economic world has developed at a rapid pace.

The encroaching globalisation of the world, the increasing necessity and use of technology, and its inherent liberalisation, have altered the way business is conducted and in so doing have affected the relationships between people and the environment.The inevitable global shift towards 'globalisation' is transforming the workplace, the job market, lifestyles, communities, industries and markets. The challenge for stakeholders involved in all industries is to find a balance between sustenance, prosperity and people's desire to improve their financial/material well-being, with the underlying need for identity, community, religion, home and family.

Travel and tourism can play a vital role in balancing these forces. It not only provides the livelihoods for both rural and urban communities, but has the capacity, when planned, developed and managed properly, to enhance community relations and build bridges of understanding and peace between nations. Travel and tourism also plays a crucial role in encouraging governments to reduce their barriers to growth.Thomas Friedman in his book *The Lexus and the Olive Tree* suggests that governments need to don a 'golden straight jacket' in order to allow pure free market capitalism and enable both developed and developing countries to achieve full economic growth within a sustainable development framework.

The first step to achieving this balance between sustainable development and economic growth for travel and tourism was in 1996.The World Travel & Tourism Council (WTTC), the World Tourism Organisation (WTO/OMT) and the Earth Council, together launched Agenda 21 for the Travel & Tourism Industry:Towards Environmentally Sustainable Development - a sectoral action plan for sustainable development based on the outcome of the Rio Earth Summit in 1992. At the time it was the only industry-specific adaptation of Agenda 21.

In 1993, according to the United Nations Statistical Commission : 'Tourism comprises the activities of persons travelling to and staying in places outside their usual environment for not more than one consecutive year for leisure, business and other purposes'.Both the inter-governmental WTO/OMT and the private sector WTTC consider the travel and tourism sector to be one of the largest -if not THE largest - in the world, particularly in terms of its contribution to the world economy. According to WTTC estimates, travel and tourism achieved the following economic impact directly and indirectly in 2001: USD3.3 trillion contribution to global GDP, almost 11% of total GDP; 207 million jobs worldwide, over 8% of all jobs; USD630 billion in capital investment, almost 9% of all capital investment.

This economic activity of the travel and tourism sector was generated by 698 million international tourist arrivals in 2000, representing an estimated 7.3% increase over 1999 according to preliminary estimates.This was the highest growth rate in nearly a decade and almost double the increase of 1999 with nearly 50 million more arrivals recorded, which is approximately what destinations such as Spain or the United States receive in the entire year. In less than a decade, international tourist arrivals are projected to reach one billion. In March 2001,WTO/OMT submitted a concise report on Sustainable Development of Tourism to the United Nations (UN), in which it noted that 'the development of tourism has been characterised by continuing geographical spread and diversification of tourist destinations. While in 1950 the top 15 tourist destinations, all in western Europe and North America, attracted 97% of the world's total arrivals, by 1999 this figure had fallen to 62%, with market shares increasing for developing countries and economies in transition, particularly in south-east Asia, central and eastern Europe, and Latin America.'

Clearly, tourists are increasingly selective about destinations and are demanding higher quality products and services. The travel and tourism industry simultaneously thrives upon this trend and is threatened by it. Tourism products and services that demonstrate 'greater sensitivity to the environment, traditional culture and local people at the destinations' can create such an experience, whereas tourism in a context of uncontrolled growth which puts increasing pressure on the natural, cultural and socioeconomic environment, risks diminishing the visitor's experience. In short, increased market demand for experiences can contribute to social, economic and environmental sustainability only if the resulting pressures from growth are properly planned and managed.

The travel and tourism industry is both receptive and conscious of the resulting pressures from economic growth and the need to protect our natural and social environment.The preservation of the tourism product—the environmental, social or cultural heritage specific to each country—is the only way to ensure a future for everyone. In response to this increase in recognition of the need to safeguard natural resources, a growing number of travel and tourism companies are seeking to create more responsible consumer behaviour by using their products and services to educate and inform their customers. Many multinational companies such as Lusotur, British Airways, Japan Travel Bureau (JTB),Taj Hotels and Preussag have all adopted 'corporate citizenship' programmes that have created dialogue between the community and the private sector, as well as promoting sustainable development.

Travel and tourism, if utilised effectively, can be a force for positive growth and economic success for both developed and developing countries. Markets have the potential to enhance lives in a sustainable framework through providing wealth creation, choice, innovation and competition.The travel and tourism industry contains these four elements that enable it to be a dynamic market force for sustainability in the future. It has the capacity to increase exports, bring in capital investment, boost an economies GDP and create employment.

Job Opportunities

Travel and tourism generates jobs throughout the economy, both in companies directly involved in the business and in related supplier industries such as retail, construction, manufacturing and telecommunications.WTTC estimated that travel and tourism generated 203 million jobs - over 8% of all jobs worldwide - in 2000, rising to over 207 million in 2001. Within a decade, this is estimated to increase to over 260 million jobs or 9% of all employment.These jobs employ a significant proportion of women, minorities and young people and are predominantly in small and medium-sized enterprises (SMEs). SMEs make up the majority of the travel and tourism sector, although the exact percentage is unknown.

SMEs encourage entrepreneurs, provide many diverse job opportunities and enable low skills entry for emerging countries. Successful human resource management, in the shape of training and education, is crucial to achieve the economic prosperity, for both SMEs and the larger multinational companies that can be accrued through tourism. Highly competitive destinations are realising that quality of services and facilities are vital to ensure a consistency of tourists to the destination. On the other hand the fragmentation of the industry and the high proportion of SMEs has led to unconstructive training and protection for employees. Given the number of low-skilled workers in the sector, the industry has been criticised for offering nothing more than 'hamburger flipping' jobs that contribute little to the sustainability of an economy or society.

The travel and tourism industry is renowned for its high turnover, anti-social working hours, low pay, seasonal employment, instability and low job status. However, this does not tell the whole story. Jobs for the Millennium—Mexico, report produced in 2000 by the WTTC and the Fundacitón Pro-Educación en Turismo, AC (FUTUR), paints a different picture of the hospitality workforce. While over 36% of the employees in over 200 companies surveyed were considered 'unskilled', almost a quarter of the jobs at these companies required professional or managerial competence, and over 45% required some level of skill.

Despite SMEs offering their employees transferable skills, there is still a considerable absence of training for these groups.There is a real need for human resource development within the sector that tackles the issues that lead to costly effects for travel and tourism. Indeed, more than a third of employers surveyed reported serious shortages of skilled workers, which would suggest that real career opportunities do exist.This has met with industry recognition of the need for human resource development that raises the industry's profile, increases productivity and provides sustainable employment.

One of the catalysts creating the urgency for trained, skilled workers within the industry is the increasing use of information technology. Travel and tourism is reliant on a human service, yet is increasingly using technology to facilitate the sector in competitive pricing.The growth in tourism forecast for the next ten years, will lead to a greater dependency on information technology, which will become more important in the future as the industry copes with rapid expansion and sophistication of the tourism and hospitality supply.

While tour operators have a limited number of staff in some of their receiving countries, a huge network of activities and jobs across the economy depends upon delivering the demand for tourism.The tour operator industries reach many areas of the economy such as hotel and infrastructure development, transport services, agriculture, information technology, restaurants and entertainment and media, education and training, consumption of pharmaceutical products, clothing, equipment, and medical services.

The hospitality industry contributes to the important process of job creation. As a labourintensive industry, it employs large numbers of wage earners, whose taxes and disposable income add to gross domestic output and help to create further employment opportunities. Given that each hotel room typically requires one member of staff, every hotel room built has the potential to create an additional job.

The bulk of cruise line employees are from countries where employment opportunities are limited and training is scarce.The industry provides the opportunity to travel, free medical care and upward mobility, particularly for women from developing nations.

Sustainable Economic Growth

In order to achieve sustainable economic growth, the travel and tourism sector needs to reduce social, economic, environmental and cultural barriers. Some of the major obstacles to this growth are the lack of infrastructure, environmental degradation and fragile linkages that weaken a country's tourism potential. One way to address these barriers is for the sector to foster tourism investment through public-private sector partnerships that not only enable a country to grow economically, but retain the essential social, cultural and environmental assets that make each country a unique product.

Public-private sector co-operation and planning are also essential to creating sustainable employment in the tourism industry, and to this end the private sector has fought for recognition of its true contribution to job growth and economic development. Hitherto, the industry had been disadvantaged by a lack of data reflecting its full economic impact. Only recently has the methodology known as Tourism Satellite Accounting (TSA), pioneered by WTTC,WTO/OMT and others, been developed and accepted by governments as a means for fully measuring travel and tourism's contribution as an economic activity. TSA is based on a 'demand-side' concept of economic activity (i.e. the economic activities of visitors and travel companies), as tourism does not supply a homogenous product or service.

Unlike traditional industries (agriculture, electronics, steel, etc.), travel and tourism is a diverse set of industries offering a multitude of products (consumer and capital durables and non-durables), and services ranging from airline and cruise ship fares and accommodations, to restaurant meals, entertainment, souvenirs and gifts, immigration and park services, recreational vehicles and automobiles, aircraft manufacturing and resort development. By using input/output modelling,TSA is able to differentiate between travel and tourism industry supply and economy supply, including that portion of supply which it imports from abroad. Additionally, it breaks down the supply side accounts into direct and indirect impacts and the individual elements of GDP (wages and salaries, transaction taxes, operating surplus, depreciation and subsidies).These data ensure governments have a broader understanding of the impact of travel and tourism, in particular the implications of policy for the travel and tourism economy.

TSA data also reiterates the fact that travel and tourism has the potential to be a catalyst industry for emerging countries to kick-start their economies, offering many opportunities that are not available in other industries. For example, the rise in cultural, heritage and wildlife niche market tourism, in developing countries, is becoming a viable alternative for communities that want to move away from mono-culture farming, which can not only destroy sustainable patterns of agriculture and traditional fertility cycles but has been associated with negative changes in social structures and economic relationships. Annual research undertaken by WTTC demonstrates that the impact of travel and tourism on the whole economy is much greater than the size of the industry itself. For every dollar spent on travel and tourism, a further dollar and a half is typically contributed to GDP in other sectors of the economy.

Tour operators can have a significant impact upon economies. Whereas the Balearic Islands were the poorest province in the whole of Spain in 1950, by the year 2000 it was the richest—almost entirely due to organised tourism. Other countries where travel and tourism has had a positive impact on the economy are the Maldives, Mexico and Turkey.

The hotel industry has considerable growth potential in those nations and regions that are just beginning to develop their economies and improve their performance, because the total output of the hotel industry is closely tied to the variables associated with economic development.These variables include basic infrastructure and levels of gross domestic output, employment, and education of the workforce.The hospitality industry also produces a 'multiplier effect' whereby money spent by hotel guests travels through a community generating further revenue.

The cruise line industry is a significant economic contributor worldwide and particularly to the United States economy, leaking into industry, agriculture, airlines, travel agents, food and beverage suppliers and other service sectors. It is also a booming industry that is forecast to grow to 20.7 million passengers by 2010.

Preserving Cultural Heritage

The mutual dependence that exists between tourism and cultural heritage is becoming more evident. While culture heritage creates a foundation for tourism's growth, tourism has the power to generate funds that make conservation possible. Cultural heritage loses much of its meaning without an audience, and a society participating in and benefiting from it. Without sustainable management, tourism loses its potential for growth. With the growing interest in culture and community, tourism is finally being recognised as an industry that can boost rural economies, create entrepreneurs and jobs and help preserve indigenous cultures. 'Above all, tourism offers a better life not just for those who make money, but for those who pay money to enjoy it'.

For example, trekking tourism has led to the transformation of the traditional subsistence farming of the Sherpas of the Khumbu region into a cash economy that has generated income, jobs and a better standard of living.One of the main challenges, therefore, for all stakeholders involved in travel and tourism, including local authorities, NGOs and businesses, is to maintain an optimal balance to ensure sustainability. Otherwise, in destinations where the natural and cultural heritage deteriorates, the economy will be put at risk as tourists migrate to better-preserved destinations.The Addo Elephant National Park in South Africa's Eastern Cape Province aimed to integrate community tourism initiatives with mainstream tourism.

A multi-stakeholder dialogue process was adopted including all private and public sector voices.The outcome was that local groups have the potential to add diversification to a primarily wildlife destination and the private sector has the key for effective marketing and business development skills. Research suggests that following the trends already mainstream in other economic sectors, social responsibility and corporate citizenship are expected to become in the future issues of strong concern requiring a response from the tourism industry as a whole, as well as at corporate level.The concept of 'corporate citizenship' is now being adopted by many of the key leaders in the private sector of travel and tourism and is emerging as a central issue for business companies.

Corporate citizenship recognises the need to create a balance between all stakeholders' needs, society's different interests and the sustainability of the natural environment with a greater focus on governance and accountability. It is about taking responsibility for, and doing as well as possible in terms of social, environmental and economic performance given competitive opportunities and constraints.The business case and corporate citizenship have become joined in current debate about the changing role of business in society.

Profit can serve many functions, and within travel and tourism modern business leaders are using it for good purposes. Multinationals can help contribute to the wealth and welfare of us all, and increasingly leading players in the travel and tourism industry are recognising the importance of the contributions they can make to the communities within which they work. Corporate citizenship balances the interests of the economy with those of public policymakers, individuals and groups in civil society. can not only improve the quality of life for distressed communities, but can also generate tangible returns for the bottom line. Within travel and tourism, corporate citizenship is becoming an increasingly important concept for the private sector.

The Tour Operators Initiative (TOI)—launched in March 2000 is a network of tour operators that have joined forces to improve their practices, as well as raise the awareness of the industry.TOI acts as a platform to develop ideas and projects to address the environmental, social, economic and cultural aspects of sustainable development within the tourism sector. Developed by tour operators, for tour operators, it has the support of UNEP, UNESCO and WTO/OMT.

Environmental Development

The travel and tourism industry has come far since the Earth Summit in Rio de Janeiro, in 1992, when the impact of industries on the environment was high on the political agenda. The increasing numbers of travellers and the rise in package tours during the 1980s were causing a valid concern among environmentalists.

WTTC, with WTO/OMT and the Earth Council, in response to the scrutiny with which tourism was judged, collaborated and produced Agenda 21 for the Travel & Tourism Industry.This public-private sector effort was designed to ensure that as travel and tourism grew globally, its influence would not have an undesirable impact on the environment. Indeed all areas of travel and tourism have over the last decade implemented many individual environmental schemes and programmes, not for-profit funds and foundations all over the world.

Recently there has also been an increase in conferences on the environment hosted by governments and by private sector companies, which are highlighting the responsibility of both the public and private sector to protect natural and cultural heritage and emphasise the importance of environmental sustainability. If tourism is not planned and managed carefully, it can overwhelm the very assets with which it attracts visitors to the destination. Examples of tourism expansion, that have ignored the local environment, are well-known: tourism facilities built on pristine land without prior consultation with the local community; golf greens that use up scarce water supplies; water pipes and infrastructure that feed major developments but often ignore the local village.

With the rise of mass tourism comes the threat of destruction of fragile eco-systems and coastal regions, local culture, and the depletion of natural resources. Conversely, tourism can generate the necessary revenue to protect and preserve biodiversity and act as a force for environmental protection especially in developing countries. Game parks and nature preserves are centres of institutional strength and can act as a focus for tourism development in rural areas.Tourism helps generate resources to maintain these protected areas, as illustrated by the Royal Chitwan National Park in Nepal, the Masai Mara in Kenyaand the rainforests of Costa Rica. Not only can it help to preserve the environment, but profits have a greater potential to reach local and rural communities, compared to other sectors.

Concept of Eco-tourism

The new concept of eco-tourism or nature tourism is experiencing faster-than-average growth. Eco-tourism alone contributed $154 billion in receipts in 2000 and is growing 20% annually compared with just 7% for tourism overallin an already booming industry, and reflects those consumers who are aware of the issues facing travel and tourism.There are indications that consumers are also beginning to influence businesses, as they become more aware of the choices available to them, and of this rapid growth in the ecotourism niche market. However, eco-tourism alone is not the answer to addressing the environmental problems facing the industry. It also remains to be seen how far consumers have the willingness to encourage businesses to adopt more sustainably-developed tourism, especially if it means paying higher prices.

Initiatives in Tourism Industry

Dialogue between stakeholders in both the private and public sectors, has led to the establishment of global voluntary initiatives throughout the last decade.These initiatives have taken various forms and represent all sectors of the travel and tourism industry. Although there has been an encouraging explosion of such schemes, adoption of them by the industry is as yet limited. It has proved particularly difficult to encourage SMEs to participate in sustainable good practice.A small sample of examples of these initiatives are given in the following paragraphs.

Awards. A number of private sector travel and tourism companies, as well as industry associations, present annual awards in recognition of outstanding actions on behalf of the environment.These include the American Society of Travel Agents and IH&RA. A number of these receive sponsorship from private sector companies such as the American Express Company.

Codes of conduct In 1992 the Pacific Asia Tourism Association (PATA) introduced its Code for Environmentally Responsible Tourism to strengthen the principles of conservation in the region, soliciting membership in its Green Leaf programme. Addressing one of the most sensitive social implications of tourism development, a multistakeholder, international public-private initiative has recently drafted the Code of Conduct for the Protection of Children from Sexual Exploitation in Travel and Tourism.

The Africa Travel Association's Responsible Traveller Guidelines and the Japanese Association of Travel Agents' Declaration of Earth Friendly Travellers are just two examples of the many industry codes aimed at educating and influencing their customers.

Green Globe 21 As a follow-up to the Earth Summit, in 1994 WTTC set up Green Globe. Now an independent private sector company, Green Globe 21 is an Agenda 21-based industry improvement programme, which provides guidance material and a certification process linked to both

ISO standards and Agenda 21 principles, throughout the world.

Dodo.The CyberDodo programme, developed by CyberDodo Productions and supported by WTTC and by the United Nations High Commissioner for Human Rights, is designed to raise awareness among adults and children of important issues concerning the environment, human rights and children's rights.The programmes have already been shown in more than 60 countries.

Green Key. Green Key, Denmark, a scheme operated by the Hotel, Restaurant and Leisure Industry Association (HORESTA) in that country, applies 78 criteria to be met by properties seeking certification.

Eco-labels. UNEP's comprehensive publication on Ecolabels in the Tourism Industry examines this form of voluntary self-regulation in the tourism industry with the aim of helping applicants to understand the nature of eco-labelling schemes.

These private sector strategies are fast becoming an essential part of the process of sustaining natural and cultural heritage because the industry has a direct impact on local communities in which they operate. Some of these programmes not only provide valuable funds to support poorer host communities, but also help encourage protection of the environment and natural resources that often get depleted by the different sectors of the industry.

Tour Operator Industry

The outbound tour operator has emerged in the past 50 years as a useful means of distributing leisure air travel and accommodation services to consumers. Consumers in one country wishing to visit another require information and want to book travel arrangements in advance.Tour operators obtain information, make contracts with suppliers of services, and publish their holiday offers in brochures, which are distributed directly to consumers or by travel agents. Tour operators judge overall demand and the expected demand for each destination and seek to satisfy that demand if it can be accomplished profitably.

Tour operators assemble the component parts of holidays. There is limited value added as reflected in profit margins that represent 1% to 2% of turnover. Present in substantial numbers in Europe (approximately 5,000) and in the United States, Canada, Japan, South Korea, Russia, Australia, New Zealand, South and Latin America, tour operators remain small in number where tourism is less developed.

Globally, they represent around 12% of international arrivals,while in Europe they account for 35% of leisure air holidays. There are five substantial European outbound tour operators, the remaining 4,995 being SMEs employing five to 100 people, which often cater for specialist interests or low volume destinations. The five large companies have integrated activities (travel agencies, tour operations, airlines, hotels, cruise ships and ground handling), but these are not exclusively used by the one integrated organisation. For example, owned airlines are used for some of the flight requirements, but large tour operators can have contracts with more than 150 airlines and owned airlines, and contract seats out to non-owned tour operators.

Tour operating employs relatively few people across the world (a few tens of thousands), but their activities can stimulate hotel and infrastructure development.These include water, sewerage, airports, roads etc, transport services, agriculture, information technology, restaurants, entertainment and media, education and training, consumption of pharmaceutical products, clothing, equipment, medical services, excursion venues and public administration concerned with policy-making, marketing and management of tourism.

While tour operators have a limited number of staff in some of their receiving countries, a huge network of activities and jobs across the economy depend upon delivering the demand for tourism.The marketing efforts of tour operators are what the suppliers of services and governments look for. The countries visited are 80% intra-regional (e.g. Germany to Spain, Australia to Thailand) and 20% long-haul (e.g. Europe to the Caribbean, Japan to Europe, the United States to Far East).Tour operators can have a significant impact upon economies. Whereas the Balearic Islands were the poorest province in the whole of Spain in 1950, by the year 2000 it was the richest - almost entirely due to organised tourism.The Maldives is no longer to be classified as a 'lesser developed country' thanks to the economic impact of tourism, particularly organised tourism.

Cancun in Mexico had a local population of 600 before tourism arrived. It now provides income for 600,000 and support for ten times that number through organised tourism from North and South America, and Europe.In Turkey, tourism revenues reach 30% of total commodity exports, most attributed to organised tourism.Foreign exchange received by countries through tour operators takes the form of payments to hotels and ground handlers as well as taxes, duties and charges. In addition, consumers spend money outside the hotel on the 'complementary offer'.This amount can vary from 150% of the hotel cost in countries such as Spain to virtually zero in those developing countries that offer little to see, do or buy.

Outbound tourism demand is affected by confidence in economic conditions and security as well as perceptions of discretionary income. Leisure outbound travel has been growing at around one and a half times the growth in GDP and is not highly volatile, unless there are safety concerns. Fluctuations in tourism revenues in receiving countries are more marked due to consumer perceptions of the relative safety and attractiveness of destinations, as well as changes in relative price.

The ability to travel and to witness other cultures not only brings prosperity to the receiving country, but also fosters understanding and tolerance in the visitor.The tour operator offer - based on high volumes, bulk buying and low prices - has provided access to travel to millions of people.The tour operator's main contribution has been to increase tourism volume in many destinations that would otherwise have had little tourism development. However, the way in which different countries and destinations have dealt with the effects of this increase varies widely.

By far the most positive influence of tourism has been on the citizens of the receiver countries, where the foreign influx has provided income for much greater social choices than have hitherto existed and accelerated the process of modernisation and openness. As local people have become richer through tourism, countries dependent on international tourism have found themselves generating a greater number of domestic tourists.The effect of this phenomenon in Spain, for example, has been the restoration of a strong Spanish identity—both cultural and culinary—which had been weakened.

Tour operator distribution has created jobs in originating countries, particularly for women in travel agencies, airlines, airports and hotels as well as for tour operators themselves. Negative social consequences have been felt in a number of different and significant ways.The 'homogenisation' of global products and services devoid of local identity has been exacerbated by tourism movements.There is no doubt that people brought for a short time to another country seek to retain their own habits and practices —while host communities adapt to satisfy visitor tastes in order to make money from them.Those with vulnerable cultures are likely to suffer most and local disaffection is most keenly felt where there are high densities of tourists. Reaction tends to come from regional, religious or cultural entities attempting to preserve key features that provide a manifestation of a local identity.

Overall, the opportunity for jobs in tourism and tourism-related activities in receiving countries have been very positive, as has the opportunity for training and development. However, a major market failure has been the inability to develop and diversify the complementary offer (things to see, buy or do outside the hotel) that would provide extra jobs and income in the community and allow monies to be distributed more widely and deeply This remains a significant opportunity to alleviate poverty in some developing countries.

In countries where the money economy is limited and unemployment high, tourism can be seen to benefit the few who are directly involved in tourism, leaving workers in the informal economy marginalised and disaffected. In addition, children vulnerable to sexual exploitation have found themselves targeted by a small number of paedophiles.

Role of Tour Operators in the Community

Tour operators have many sub-contracted suppliers that are expected to deliver quality services under some form of supervision.They rely upon close relationships with people working in the destinations—at airports, hotels, restaurants, excursion venues, public administrations, medical authorities, etc.—for without them, holidays could not be delivered. Tour operators have resident staff, or those of their local agents that maintain these relationships and are expected to become familiar with concerns expressed by local communities.

Where good quality accommodation for customers is in short supply, many tour operators co-finance developments on a short-term basis. Tour operators act as a bridge between suppliers, customers and the country visited, providing information about the destination, safety and cultural sensitivity (dress codes, etc). With smaller guided tours, customers often seek greater detailed interaction and are very aware of their social and cultural responsibilities.

Role of the IFTO

The International Federation of Tour Operators (IFTO) acts as the spokesperson for tour operators (and their clients) with municipalities, regional and national governments and international organisations such as the WTO/OMT, UNCTAD,WHO, UNESCO, UNEP, and the EU. Issues range from the broadest level (e.g. Code of Ethics of Tourism at WTO/OMT) to the narrowest (e.g. provision of clean water to particular hotels or districts). Its dealings with the public administration involve ministries of foreign affairs, home affairs, public works, environment, transport, tourism, education, health and finance. In the private sector, all the actors in tourism and related to tourism are involved in discussions. As tourism is a horizontal activity, co-ordination, consultation and partnerships (public-public, private-private and public-private partnerships) are essential for it to be successful.

Environmental Impact

The direct environmental impact of tour operators is relatively limited, but there are ways in which they can have a positive influence.Tour operators communicate with customers mainly through paper-based media, therefore brochures need to be used efficiently and to be sourced from renewable forests and recycled whenever possible. Offices need to consume as little energy as possible and customers need to be encouraged to make choices and to behave in ways that are socially and environmentally acceptable.

In considering the indirect effects of tour operators encouraging people to travel, a distinction needs to be made between developed and developing nations when considering environmental action. Developed nations have the technical and financial resources to monitor and enforce environmental standards in tourism development and, in many cases, the political will to act as well as a body of planning regulations. In these circumstances, should a problem arise (e.g. an individual hotel failing to perform at the level required) a basis for negotiation exists between the governing authorities and the local tourism actors together with IFTO.

Developing countries may have priorities that are more pressing than sustainable development in tourism.There may be neither the political will nor the technical or financial resources to monitor environmental performance. In these situations it is important for the tour operator and other tourism actors to adopt self-regulation. For example, in the Antarctic where no legal framework exists and the environment is highly vulnerable, tour operators and cruise ships have signed up to a defined code of conduct.This is weaker than a legal solution as no effective sanctions can be applied to those not adhering to the code.

Energy consumption/emissions

Tour operators encourage people to travel from their local airport, which usually means a taxi or a car journey. Airports have been extended as a result of consumer demand - larger aircraft are now used.Tour operators seek out the lowest seat mile costs—this requires in turn, high-density seating and fuel-efficient modern aircraft operating at high load factors.The resulting emissions of noise, CO_2 and NO_x per passenger are lower than for other forms of aviation, but nonetheless would not have occurred had customers stayed at home.

Customers are usually transported from the destination airport to the hotel by modern diesel-engined or gas-powered coaches which can carry up to 58 people and have low seat/mile CO_2 emissions.These vehicles reduce the incidence of car traffic by more than 25 times. However, in many developing countries these are not available; LPG (liquid petroleum gas) or CNG (compressed nitrogen gas) distribution is extremely limited. While at the hotel, visitor energy consumption/ emissions due to air-conditioning is broadly equivalent to energy consumption/emissions through central heating at home unless, as in Cyprus, all tourist establishments are required to install solar panels, in which case energy consumption by tourists will be less than that by residents. In beach destinations where movement outside hotels is limited to excursions, consumption/emissions during a two-week stay are likely to be much less than staying at home.

Water Consumption

The huge majority of tourists fly from colder to warmer climates in countries with beaches nearer the equator, which get less rain and have less available water. Although tourism uses very little water compared with agriculture, there is a significant increase in the consumption of water as a result of tourism. De-salination plants have been installed in some areas of high-density tourism where there are water shortages. Hotels pay for water consumption by volume and this is reflected in prices to consumers. Many hotels employ systems (including incentives for customers) to reduce consumption of water and energy consumption and waste, but this remains a major issue in much of the developed and developing world.

Waste management

Sewerage systems are expensive and 'high tech' systems are required to avoid contamination of seawater.These may be funded through central/local government and through multi-lateral sources. Huge investments have taken place in coastal areas of high tourism density, but much remains to be done. Likewise, solid waste is a major issue for many municipalities operating in tourism areas.

Planning regulations

Where construction of airports, roads, hotels and other infrastructure is concerned, planning regulations that determine maximum spread and density are required to maintain an appropriate balance.Where local governance is weak there are frequent examples of over development.The degradation of heritage sites that suffer from visitor congestion is another issue, which has yet to be dealt with satisfactorily.

Areas for Improvement

Key areas for improvement include:

— tour operators need to develop a responsible tourism policy;

— better information to consumers from tour operators, particularly on credible environmental standards applied to and monitored among sub-contracted suppliers;

— stronger relationships with tour operators and local public-private sector actors in all significant tourism destinations to support destination management policies aimed at sustainable development.This should lead to constructive consultation as well as the emergence of true local partnerships;

— significant development of the 'complementary offer' to create jobs among women and the local community in developing countries, and greater development of local agriculture to provide specific foods for tourists;

— encouragement of zero-emission terrestrial vehicles and aircraft;

— management of water, waste and energy consumption and the protection of tourism sites (heritage and natural) from unmanaged tourism flows that degrade both the natural environment and the visitor experience;

- encourage tour operators to adopt selfregulation through appropriate codes of conduct specific to habitat and destination where there are insufficient governance and institutional frameworks;
- raising tour operators' awareness of the social dimension of sustainable development and ensuring that policies and communications to consumers reflect local community concerns;
- tour operators need to ensure those sustainable tourism development concepts, procedures and practices are included in their management and representative training programmes;
- tour operators need to set goals for sustainable development against which their performance can be measured and reported both internally and publicly.

Methods of Implementation

Tour operators use a variety of tools to create feedback systems to alert the tour operators as well as public and private actors in the destinations.

- TUI, a part of Preussag, one of the largest tour operators in the world, with 23 million customers, and Scandinavian Leisure Group, part of MyTravel, track the environmental performance of destinations and sub-contracted suppliers;
- many of the small tour operators have clear guidelines for their staff to follow and report back on adverse consequences of their tourism activity. Customers, too, are quick to bring to the attention of tour operators' adverse consequences. NGOs can also contribute their views;

- the issues raised are commonly dealt with through the local contacts of tour operators in the destination. Otherwise, in a destination with high volumes of tourists, IFTO is often used to communicate the adverse consequences and recommend remedial action;
- more recently, the Tour Operator Initiative (under the aegis of UNEP, UNESCO and WTO/OMT) has provided the beginnings of a network of tour operators large and small, to develop better policies and systems of implementation;
- IFTO has played an active and prominent role with WTO/OMT by chairing its Business Council. Sustainable development is a key part of WTO/OMT's programme of work.

Tour operators should set the goal of introducing a comprehensive responsible tourism policy covering direct action and indirect impacts, within the next five years.

Tour operators direct action:

- better information to consumers;
- more use of electronic communication;
- reduction in use of paper;
- better use of recycled paper and paper from renewable forests;
- eliminate use of toxic paper coating;
- aggregate performance data to support corporate annual reporting and year on year improvements,
- ensure that sustainable development concepts, procedures and practices are included in management and representative training programmes;
- ensure greater adherence to tour operator codes of conduct.

Success in the above areas will depend on:

— the development of agreed international criteria against which to measure the environmental performance of subcontracted suppliers in order to keep consumers better informed;

— the extent of the use of electronic means of communication;

— technological innovation and progress that will allow the development of low cost, thin (low weight) shiny paper for brochures that have high levels of environmental performance.

Indirect impacts:

— tour operators need to improve their monitoring of the social and environmental performance of sub-contracted suppliers and destinations (building on health and safety initiatives and guidelines);

— tour operators should develop stronger relationships with local public and private sector actors in all significant tourism destinations, to support destination management policies and strategies aimed at sustainable development (multistakeholder involvement).

In addition, tour operators need to:

— protect the natural environment and cultural heritage,

— conserve plants and animals, protected areas and landscapes,

— respect the integrity of local cultures and their social institutions.

Incoming tour Operators

Most international visitors are unfamiliar with the countries they visit.To assist them plan and operate their itineraries, hotels, visits and attractions, the role of the incoming tour operator, agent or groundhandler has emerged. Many are simply organised as a service to customers, others have broadened the scope of their activities through backward integration by buying coach companies and hotels. With the emergence of outbound tour operators, the role of the incoming tour operator has been much enhanced. Contracts are made between the two to deliver transfers and excursions and (on occasions) hotels.The incoming tour operator provides all logistical support as well as providing local knowledge (commercial, legal, political and environmental) on what can and cannot be done.

Very few incoming tour operators have been acquired by outbound tour operators, and 99% remain as local independent businesses. Worldwide there are many thousands of incoming tour operators. In developing countries, in particular, these local businesses compete to represent tour operators and those that fail resent that all the business of the outbound tour operator goes through one local business.

The incoming tour operator attempts to create a range of offers to attract consumers that are practical in terms of logistics and the environment and provide the right price/ value to consumers and profits to themselves. From the perspective of the suppliers in the receiving destination, the incoming tour operator forms part of their destination network for which they are prepared to pay. The outbound tour operator can also play a role in that distribution to customers.

The coach companies play a crucial role in the batch distribution of customers from airport to hotels and on tours to excursion venues. Their fleets are, in the main, very modern and well maintained.The rent-a-car companies usually provide new or nearly new vehicles for hire.The economic value of rent-a-cars for tourism is that customers can reach destinations not accessible without motorised transport. The major attractions act as magnets to tourists providing the motivation for visits and leading to increased use of hotel rooms, roads, airports, rail transport as well as the land use for the attraction itself.They can provide a major drive for increased local employment.

The incoming tour operators can, and do, lay down clear policies and procedures for subcontracted suppliers to follow to protect the environment (for example, relating to driving on safari in Africa) and to support enlightened social policies, (portering in mountainous areas in south-east Asia). However, these local businesses are run on local labour law, regulations, custom and practice. In some developing countries, the custom andb practice may not meet the standards demanded, for example, by International Labour Organization (ILO).

Outbound tour operators can have influence over how their passengers are handled by the incoming tour operators/suppliers, however, they have no influence on how the incoming tour operator arranges for the majority of their work with their suppliers that takes place with individuals on independently organised groups. The incoming tour operators recognise that they have a significant role to play in tourism development.Their decisions on excursion venues and planning of trips can have strong impacts on particular communities.These communities are in competition with each other for offering attractions to tourists who have limited time (e.g. craft markets).

Tourists will often go to one craft market, but not two, so decisions by incoming tour operators count heavily. The obligation of the coach companies is to ensure that the vehicles are safe and secure and emit the lowest emissions possible with the use of local fuels.Their social obligations relate to conditions of work, particularly drivers' hours, as well as driving and parking procedures. The major attractions can be of cultural heritage e.g. Karnak,Taj Mahal, or can be recently man-made e.g. Disney or Universal Studios.

The attractions of cultural heritage can lead to excessive use and congestion and to environmental degradation.The man-made attractions have imposed upon them a panoply of planning and social regulation with which to comply.This includes stringent environmental impact assessments before any project is finally approved.

The challenges for incoming tour operators, agents and groundhandlers are:

— to obtain from government recognition of their influential role,

— to take a balanced and responsible approach to the provision of services that they provide within the context and possibilities of their local conditions,

— to influence their subcontracted suppliers to adopt a similar balanced responsible approach.

Hospitality Industry: A Dynamic Component of the Tourism Industry

The hospitality sector (i.e. hotels and restaurants) is an essential and dynamic component of the world's largest industry - travel and tourism.The global hotel industry covers a wide range of accommodation services from full-service luxury hotels to bed and breakfast operations, inns, all-suite hotels, and limited service and economy properties. These establishments may be owned and/or managed by independent operators, multinational chains, insurance companies, pension funds, governments and other investors.

The International Hotel & Restaurant Association (IH&RA) as the sole trade association exclusively dedicated to representing the hospitality industry at the international level, is also the only body to have attempted to quantify the size and scale of the sector on a global basis. The largest concentration of hotels in the European Economic Area

(EEA) with 159,226 properties, followed by the North American region, with just over 65,000 hotels.This contrasts sharply, for instance, with South Asia, which, with 15,066 hotel properties, represents less than 1% of total world supply.An industry of such magnitude inevitably has far-reaching impacts of a social, economic and environmental nature, as was confirmed by the second IH&RA White Paper.This found that sustainable development and social issues had become key forces driving change in the multinational hospitality industry and an important yardstick against which the industry's development will be measured in the near future.

Although industry consolidation is a continuing trend, the hospitality sector is still predominantly made up of small and mediumsized enterprises (SMEs). Research indicates that approximately 20% of hotels worldwide are branded (i.e. have an affiliation to a national or international chain of hotels), and 80% are independent, although the ratio of branded to non-branded hotels in the United States is higher (70/30), a trend which Europe is likely to follow —albeit at a slower pace—given the existing low level of brand penetration and continued high volumes expected in international travel.

Given its size and scope, the international hospitality industry makes a major contribution to gross domestic output. In both developing nations (where tourism may be the primary industry) and developed countries, industry revenues constitute an important part of the local and national economy.They do so via four major activities, profits earned and distributed to owners, taxes paid on sales, wages and real estate, jobs created; and purchases of supplies and materials. Industry taxation generates significant funding for governments.This in turn, is used to provide services for citizens and travellers. As well as income tax, hotels pay business taxes, licence fees and real estate taxes, in addition to the social charges often imposed on employee wages. Being such an important source of tax revenue, hotels can be viewed as highly productive members of the economic community, compared with other property investments that do not provide this multiple taxing opportunity.

Hotels and restaurants also contribute to the important process of job creation. As a labourintensive industry, hospitality employs large numbers of wage earners, whose taxes and disposable income add to gross domestic output and help to create further employment opportunities. Given that each hotel room typically requires one member of staff, every hotel room built has the potential to create an additional job.Furthermore, for every dollar spent by a guest in a hotel, one additional revenue dollar is generated for the community. Referred to as the 'multiplier effect', this concept is used by economists to explain how money spent by a hotel guest travels through a community to purchase the goods and services required to meet the guest's needs.

In the United States, for example, the multiplier effect is approximately two; that is, for every dollar spent by a guest in a hotel, one additional revenue dollar is generated across a wide range of businesses.The total output of the hotel industry is closely tied to the variables associated with economic development such as basic infrastructure and levels of Gross Domestic Product (GDP), employment and education of the workforce.This relationship is worth noting since it can be expected that the hotel industry has considerable growth potential in those nations and regions that are just beginning to fully develop their economies and improve their performance in each macroeconomic variable.

Of particular concern to the hospitality industry in high-income countries are current demographic trends - notably declining birth rates and ageing populations - which put further pressure on an industry characterised by high turnover and a shortage of qualified labour in both developed and developing countries.These problems are exacerbated by constraints on the international mobility of workers as a result of visa restrictions and national immigration quotas.

By providing many young or unskilled people with their first job experience, the industry also effectively offers them an entry into the labour market.The industry's labour-intensive nature puts it in a prime position to draw upon all sectors of society to meet its workforce needs. It is worth noting that in some countries women account for up to 70% of all employees in the catering and accommodation sector, according to estimates by the International Labour Organization (ILO).Given its key contribution to gross global output and employment generation, and the social consequences this may have, hospitality industry leaders are being challenged to demonstrate greater levels of social responsibility and will be increasingly called upon to address the gap between the so-called 'haves' and 'have-nots'.

In this spirit, some hotel companies have signed agreements with trade unions, which focus on issues of trade union rights, skills training and equality in the workplace. Noting that 'in the global economy, all social and economic progress is contingent upon the maintaining of a society based on democratic values and respect for human rights', the Accor Group and the International Union of Food, Agricultural, Hotel, Restaurant, Catering, Tobacco and Allied Workers' Associations (IUF) have undertaken to respect ILO conventions relating to:

— the right of employees to affiliate to the union of their choice,
— the protection of employees against all acts of discrimination that tend to violate freedom of association,
— the protection of employees against any measures that could harm them as a result of them being union representatives.

There is also growing pressure on the multinational industry to plough more of its wealth back into those parts of the developing world where it operates. In an era when wealth sharing can be achieved through joint venture schemes or other forms of ownership, the expectation is that all stakeholders in a hotel project (be they investors, employees, or government) should have an equitable share in the profits. Increasingly, criticism is directed at governments that remove all forms of financial obstacles as an incentive to hotel companies to locate within their borders.

The challenge of the shrinking labour pool is compounded by pandemic HIV/AIDS particularly for hotels located in high-risk areas where the disease is widespread. An actuarial study of South Africa, for example, revealed that the transport, catering and accommodation sectors are the most at risk from the epidemic with an estimated 26% of the region's hospitality workforce ultimately becoming infected.Yet the problem is by no means exclusive to sub-Saharan Africa and its implications extend well beyond the labour supply.

Hotels increasingly recognise the need for measures to protect 'frontline' employees given the higher-than-average extent of direct contact between customers and staff. One response to this need has been the publication of the Guide for the Hospitality Industry on dealing with HIV/AIDS in the Workplace produced by IH&RA in collaboration with UNAIDS.This gives guidance to hotels on introducing an AIDS policy and AIDS education in the workplace and details essential safety measures (treating injuries, disposing of syringes and razors etc.).

The commercial sexual exploitation of children in tourism - commonly referred to as child sex tourism - is a further area of social concern with implications not just for hotels worldwide, but for the tourism industry as a whole. No matter how inadvertently, hotels along with other tourism operators may be implicated. Experience in the field shows that this is one area where collaboration between the various private sector partners, national governments and their law-enforcing agencies is vital.

IH&RA, for example, is an active member of the international steering committee on the Code of Conduct for the Protection of Children from Sexual Exploitation in Travel and Tourism, together with other stakeholders, including Interpol,WTO, the Tourism Authority of Thailand (TAT), and other representatives from the tourism industry.

Protecting the Environment

As a major component of travel and tourism, the hospitality industry (characteristically a private sector activity involving SMEs widely dispersed across the local environment) has a vested interest in protecting the environment - its key resource. Individual operators and major hospitality chains alike are increasingly hearing this message as they implement environmentallyfriendly energy conservation and waste disposal measures tailored to their specific needs.

Indeed, by the very nature of their operations, hotels are likely to take a multitude of environmental actions that extend beyond the control of any single monitoring agency.As a result, self-regulation appears to be the most viable course of action, whether in the form of in-house environmental audits, the adoption of an environmental management system, and/or application for eco-certification such as Green Leaf, Green Key or Green Globe issued by one of a number of recognised bodies.

Indeed, the moral, social and political arguments for conducting business in an environmentally-sound manner are becoming more and more widely accepted.This is particularly noteworthy given the potential impacts the industry can have on air quality, energy and water consumption, land use and waste generation. Although less 'polluting' than some other industries such as certain manufacturing processes, hospitality businesses, like most others, contribute to emissions into the atmosphere (through the use of fossil fuels and ozone-depleting substances and the transportation of supplies).

The hospitality industry can also be considered a significant user of energy in the form of heat and power. As this directly involves the burning of fossil fuels and the emission of greenhouse gases, the hospitality industry is also an indirect contributor to global warming. As a result, industry bodies regularly draw attention to the importance of eliminating ozone-depleting substances in refrigeration, air-conditioning and fire-extinguishing appliances to avoid further contributing to this phenomenon.

Water is perhaps the hospitality industry's most important resource.Tourists typically consume considerably more water than local residents. A hotel can consume between 60m3 and 220m3 per guest room per year depending on the facilities provided and whether sound water conservation practices are in place, such as water flow restrictors and on-site waste water treatment facilities.

Major efforts have been made by the industry to disseminate information and advice on these and other resource and energy-saving measures, including several produced jointly by IH&RA and partner organisations.Hotel developments can hasten the installation of much-needed water, power and transport infrastructure.

Hospitality developers are well aware that poor siting, design, engineering and construction of tourism facilities run counter to their long-term interests by causing erosion, landslides and flooding. Much has been learnt from past experience, including the importance of preserving natural protective features such as dunes and vegetation cover when constructing hotel facilities on the waterfront in low-lying and coastal areas, and of harmoniously integrating hospitality facilities with the natural or architectural features of the surrounding area.Constructing or refurbishing hotels can be an opportunity to apply traditional techniques and technologies, to rediscover local materials, and to consult with local communities to learn how best to construct buildings that respect a given landscape and suit a particular climate.

The control of environmental impacts also depends on a strong local government capable of enforcing building and planning regulations.This is particularly important at a time when tourism and hospitality businesses continue to expand into remote areas. Most hotels generate large quantities of solid waste including bottles and food packaging, kitchen and garden waste, old furniture and equipment and potentially hazardous wastes such as asbestos and solvents.

Waste disposal costs money and for this reason, hotels are increasingly careful to reduce waste volumes because it makes sound business sense.They do so by minimising the materials used in the first place, recycling and reusing waste materials wherever possible, and by safely disposing of residual wastes.The Orchid Hotel in Mumbai, India, provides a particularly good example of innovative recycling and waste disposal.Virtually all in-room products are reusable or recyclable, paper usage is kept to a minimum and kitchen waste is composted in on-site vermiculture pits.

As a major consumer of goods and services, the industry has a strong impact on the supply chain and can induce better environmental practices here.Through their collective efforts hospitality businesses can contribute to increasing recycling volumes, driving down recycling costs, increasing the profitability of local recycling markets and raising customer awareness. Hospitality services people at leisure—who offer a captive audience for environmental communication.

Many tourists feel good knowing that they have spent a low-impact holiday and used the services of environmentconscious operators.The feel-good factor is not limited to tourists - it can also extend to employees. In fact, good environmental stewardship has been found to reduce employee turnover, and motivate employees to become environment-conscious citizens.

Growth of Education Programmes and Training

IH&RA, in conjunction with partners such as UNEP-DTIE, the International Hotels Environment Initiative (IHEI), the UNAIDS programme and its member national hospitality associations, has sought to raise industry awareness of the social, economic and environmental dimensions of sustainable development through numerous educational programmes and publications. As indicated above, in the social domain, IH&RA has collaborated with UNAIDS to produce a manual addressing the issue of HIV/AIDS in the workplaceand has actively participated in WTO's campaign against Child Sex Tourism by publishing practical advice for hoteliers on how to deter this form of criminal activity and where to get help.

At the corporate level, many global hospitality companies are also involved in a range of voluntary initiatives. Marriott International, for instance, has committed to assisting the communities in which it operates, believing that business enterprises should be active in supporting community concerns. In the specifically environmental domain, curriculum materials for hotel schools recently developed by IH&RAdemonstrate that sound environmental policy is not limited to one geographical region, nor is it the exclusive preserve of multinational companies—independent hotels have also shown outstanding leadership here.

Given the predominance of SMEs in the hospitality sector, legislative enforcement and verification of compliance with environmental measures is highly complex.Therefore, voluntary initiatives such as eco-labels, environment awards and codes of conduct are proving to be an effective method of encouraging environmental improvement across a large number of businesses. In response to growing consumer awareness of the environmental context when purchasing products, eco-labelling has been one of the most successful means for a hotel to gain environmental credibility and custom.

Certification may originate within a national hotel association, such as the Hotel Association of Canada's Green Leaf programme, as a joint initiative between the national hotel association and other local tourism partners, such as HORESTA's Green Key programme in Denmark, and Green Globe 21 supported by WTTC and other key international players. Or, finally, it may be devised by a consulting firm such as the HVS Ecotel certification programme. In order to obtain an eco-label, a hotel must be independently audited on a regular basis to ensure it meets standards and policies relating to a general code of conduct or specific benchmark.

According to the Caribbean Alliance for Sustainable Tourism (CAST), an environmental initiative run by the Caribbean Hotel Association for the benefit of its member hotels, the eco-label certification process has not only created a competitive advantage for many hoteliers, but has also directly benefited the bottom line. Routine measures can reduce water consumption and related costs by up to 30%, provide significant savings in energy, solid waste haulage, chemical and maintenance costs, and have a typical payback period of less than two years.

Other advantages frequently include a positive impact on corporate/hotel image, internal management, local community relations, client satisfaction (reported to be 90% under Costa Rica's Certification for Sustainable Tourism), and reduced environmental liability. In terms of the hospitality industry's social contribution, one initiative particularly worth noting is the Singapore-based Pan Pacific Hotel & Resort's Youth Career Initiative. Launched with support from the United Nations Children's Fund (UNICEF) at the Pan Pacific Hotel in Bangkok in 1995, this IH&RA-endorsed programme offers severely under-privileged young people a 20-week training course in basic life skills along with an introduction to the hospitality industry. It seeks to open up genuine career opportunities that will lift them out of poverty and protect them from prostitution.

The programme has now been set up in Manila (Philippines), Jakarta (Indonesia) and Dhaka (Bangladesh) and will be extended to other world regions such as Africa, Latin America and the Caribbean in the near future. To date, over 400 young people have benefited from the programme, some even using it as the stepping-stone to higher education. On the cultural side, IH&RA has partnered with the United Nations Educational, Scientific and Cultural Organisation (UNESCO) in a joint initiative encouraging hotel companies to invest in the archaeological and cultural heritage on which cultural tourism thrives. Major hotel chains participating in this 'Memories of the Future' programme have financially supported restoration and enhancement projects for UNESCO World Heritage Sites such as Prince Gong's Palace, Beijing and the Medina of Tunis (Accor) or the historic City of Krakow in Poland, the City of Tyre in Lebanon and the Bahla Fort in Oman.

Multi-stakeholder Communication

Hospitality companies, like all businesses, answer to a variety of stakeholders, including investors, customers, employees, suppliers and the local community. Increasingly, they are experiencing demand for greater participation in decision-making by representatives of the latter category, which may translate into a heightened need to obtain voter approval for planning and development, for example, by carrying-out an environmental impact assessment. In this new regulatory context, corporations are being pressured into making a higher community commitment through charitable involvement, a trend mirrored in the corporate marketing techniques increasingly used for the generation of brand awareness.

Exemplary instances of local community consultation can be found in both the independent and chain hotel sector. Facing the threat of becoming an island of conserved habitat in a sea of rural poverty, the Phinda Mountain & Forest Lodge, in South Africa, has made a commitment to ensure the local community draws sustained benefits from its natural resources. Radisson SAS has established its Responsible Business Agenda for key stakeholder groups (including suppliers, local communities, media and environmental representatives) to determine what they can rightfully expect from the company.

Both companies recognise the role of key stakeholders in the decision-making process. Beyond these individual examples and others like them, however, further research must be conducted to track what the industry is doing as a whole in regard to communicating and consulting with its stakeholders.

The ever-increasing pressure from hotel stakeholders for transparency and openness about the broader environmental aspects of hospitality operations is reflected in a widespread trend towards environmental reporting among hotels. Company environmental reports are considered an excellent means for self-assessment - by monitoring progress and measuring the results achieved. Indeed, environmental reporting is starting to evolve into 'sustainability reporting' which communicates the economic performance of the company, and its environmental and social impacts.

Moreover, financial institutions have come to regard sustainable principles and practices as fundamental to sound business management, giving companies that wish to be considered 'responsible' an additional incentive to monitor, measure and report performance in the future.Accordingly, more and more multinational hotel companies are reporting their environmental activities and performance on regular basis.

Implementation of the Rio principles

IH&RA has been instrumental in advocating the implementation of the Rio principles in the hospitality industry through its ongoing efforts to raise environmental awareness. With WTTC, it participated in the 7th Session of the United Nations Commission on Sustainable Development, which focused for the first time on tourism. In particular IH&RA and WTTC co-ordinated industry representation at the multi-stakeholder dialogue on tourism.

Cruise Line Industry

The passenger cruise industry is an exciting, modern and rapidly expanding global industry. During the current decade, it has continued to expand its capacity and to develop new cruising opportunities for vacationers.The growth and global reach has been exceptional for an industry with such high capital costs, and with such a complex regulatory and legal environment in which to operate.

With capacity projected to continue to increase each year, the future offers extraordinary opportunities for the industry, its customers and suppliers.This increase in capacity is driven by a record number of new ships coming into service. Among these will be mega-liners that can accommodate more than 3,000 passengers as well as smaller, more intimate luxury vessels.The industry has a history of growth approaching 8% per year for the past decade, and the outlook for the future seems extremely bright.

According to a recent study conducted by analyst G.P. Wild,total cruise passengers are forecasted to grow from 9.8 million last year to 20.7 million by 2010. Within these figures, the North American market will go up from 6.8 million to 11.9 million and mainland Europe will grow from 1.3 million to 5.3 million. In sum, the passenger cruise industry is a dynamic sector of the global economy.

ICCL is the leading trade association that represents the interests of the 16 largest passenger cruise lines that handle 95% of the North American vacation cruise market and approximately 85% worldwide. It also represents a growing number of over 73 strategic cruise industry business partners. In 2002, the member lines of ICCL will sail over 90 vessels and will carry more than seven million passengers. The mission of ICCL is to participate in the international and United States regulatory and policy development process and ensure that all measures adopted provide for a safe, secure and healthy cruise ship environment.

Under the direction of the chief executives of its member lines, ICCL advocates industry positions to key domestic and International regulatory organisations, policy-makers and other industry partners. ICCL actively monitors domestic and international shipping policy and regulations and develops recommendations for its membership on a wide variety of issues, including safety, public health, environmental protection, security, medical facilities, and passenger protection. Conferred the status of a non-governmental consultative organisation to the International Maritime Organisation (IMO), ICCL actively participates in reviewing current maritime issues and developing conventions and treaties which, when adopted and ratified by member nations, become international law. Through IMO, maritime nations have developed consistent and uniform international standards that apply to all vessels engaged in international commerce.These standards are set forth in a number of conventions and codes such as:

— SOLAS (Safety of Life at Sea);
— STCW (Standards of Training, Certification and Watchkeeping);
— MARPOL (Marine Prevention of Pollution from Ships);
— ISM (International Safety Management Code).

International conventions set the benchmark for environmental and safety standards throughout the world. As an NGO, ICCL actively contributes to the deliberations of the Maritime Safety Committee (MSC), the Marine Environment Protection Committee (MEPC) and the numerous sub-committees, working groups and correspondence groups through submission of reports and papers, participation in discussion, and correspondence groups. ICCL is an active participant in the development and fine-tuning of these important international regulatory regimes that apply throughout the world.

The countries where vessels are registered or 'flagged' have the responsibility to oversee compliance with the internationally agreedupon requirements established by these and other treaties. Additionally, a port state, such as the United States, provides additional oversight regarding compliance and exercises jurisdiction over vessels while they operate within the waters of that coastal nation. While operating within United States waters, laws such as the Resource Conservation and Recovery Act, the Clean Air Act, the Clean Water Act, the Refuse Act and the Federal Water Pollution Control Act apply.The United States Coast Guard enforces both international requirements and the United States domestic laws with regard to cruise ships operating within their jurisdiction. ICCL works with leading flag and port state administrations, international shipping associations and classification societies on safety, security and environmental issues. ICCL constantly strives to improve safety procedures, and the excellent safety record of ICCL member operators attests to the proactive steps taken by these operators to safeguard their passengers and crews, and their commitment to provide a safe, clean and fair work environment for their on-board personnel.

ICCL's commitment to excellence is also demonstrated by its readiness to work with, and to initiate partnerships with various United States government agencies. ICCL currently has a formal partnership agreement with the United States Coast Guard and a Memorandum of Understanding (MOU) with the Florida Department of Environmental Protection (FL DEP). ICCL also works closely with the United States EPA, other state and federal agencies and public advocacy groups to address safety, security, health and environmental protection concerns.

During the last decade, the cruise ship business is a tourist industry that has grown rapidly. According to WTO, world demand reached 8.7 million passengers in 1999.The North American markets cover two-thirds of the global volume, this is primarily due to the renaissance of the cruising destinations in the Caribbean. Although the number is relatively small in the global holiday market, the industry has an enormous momentum and it is believed that North American and European demand will, by the end of 2010, surpass 12 million passengers.

In the North American market, the United States is the dominant source of cruise passengers. However, in recent years a growing percentage of passengers have come from Europe, Canada, and other areas.This expansion has led to cruise line employment of men and women in these markets both ashore and aboard ships. Comparing 1998 to 1990, cruise ship embarkation from North American ports increased by almost 70 %.The major United States ports of call are located in Florida, Alaska, California, Louisiana, New York, Texas and Massachusetts.

In Florida alone, over 3.2 million passengers embarked from the ports of Miami, Everglades, Canaveral, Palm Beach and Tampa in 2001. An additional 1.1 million passengers also boarded in San Juan, Puerto Rico and non-US ports, primarily Vancouver and Montreal (Canada). Globally, while the Caribbean region is the principal destination with 44.5% share of placement, a significant percentage of the global capacity is allocated to other markets. These include Alaska, 7.9%, the Mediterranean, 12.7%, Europe, 8.1%, the Trans-Canal (Panama), 4.0%, United States West Coast, 3.3%, Hawaii, 2.6%, and South America, 2.4%.

Among the remaining destinations, the capacity for world, Transatlantic, Asia, Australia, Middle East and Antarctica cruises has more than doubled since 1990.The social, environmental and economic sectors of these emerging destinations will prove to be a challenge and an opportunity.The cruise industry has developed into a significant economic contributor to the United States economy, including industry, agriculture, and the service sector.A study conducted in 2001 by the Business Research and Economic Advisors (BREA)concluded that in 2000, total economic benefit by the cruise industry and cruise-related activities was approximately USD17.9 billion. Of this, the cruise industry contributed USD9.4 billion in direct spending for the products and services of United States companies.

The industry's extensive economic relationships include high-tech equipment, travel services, banking and insurance, textiles, technical services, dry-docking and shipyard repair. Other major United States industries that benefit from the cruise business are the airlines, travel agents, food and beverage suppliers and the business and service sectors. Total wages generated for United States employees was USD8.7 billion. As a result of these economic partnerships, the cruise industry is able to create employment for thousands of United States citizens and support for state and local economies in all 50 states.The BREA study estimates that in 2000, the cruise industry generated jobs for 257,067 Americans.

In the United States, capital expenditures by the cruise lines more than doubled between 1997 and 2000. According to BREA, this growth required significant investment in new cruise ships and upgrading of the existing fleet. Other purchases by the cruise lines rose 30%. In total, spending in the United States associated with the industry increased by nearly a third between 1997 and 2000, to USD9.4 billion. While these economic benefits in the United States are substantial, there are also significant benefits worldwide in the industry's new emerging markets.

By way of example, the cruise industry has significant impact in Germany, Finland and Italy due to the shipbuilding activities in those nations. In nations where tourism is encouraged, the cruise lines purchased services ashore (transportation, tour operations, supplies, etc) and many of the service sectors and local business benefit from cruise ship tourists spending ashore. Moreover, tourism activity can lead to development of new markets for the products of local artisans, which not only has both the social and economic benefit of additional local income, but also helps preserve cultural tradition and identity.Although there has been some concern that these economic gains in tourist destinations are seasonal, it is clear that the markets involved are better off with the cruise industries financial input, and sufficient growth can more than compensate for the seasonal variation.

The cruise industry brings a burgeoning tourism economy to many ports around the world.The importance of the social and economic opportunities cannot be understated. It has an effect on all sectors in the port city and country.The cruise lines' presence, even on a seasonal basis, in port cities strengthens the economy for many local elements. In addition to local port user fees and head taxes and surcharges, cruise ships purchase supplies and services such as pilots, tugboats, waste disposal services, fuel and fresh water at ports of call worldwide.

Visits by cruise ships generate hundreds of millions of dollars worth of business to attractions, restaurants, retail shops, shore tour operators and other businesses at ports of call. From local artisans and craftsmen to infrastructure development such as transportation, all benefit from the expenditures of the tourists that cruise ships provide. In some instances, foreign ports that the cruise industry decides to visit become an economic stimulus for host countries to develop tourism and destination development programmes, involving local participation in providing goods and services.

A 2001 study conducted for the Florida-Caribbean Cruise Association (FCCA) by PricewaterhouseCoopers (PwC) and BREAfound that during the 1999/2000 cruise year in the Caribbean, a typical cruise ship carrying 2,000 passengers and 900 crew members generated an average of $260,000 in passenger and crew expenditures during an average port-of-call visit.

Cruise lines are continuously reviewing existing ports of call for tour operation capabilities, investment opportunities for development and upgrades to passenger terminal facilities, and total customer satisfaction of the cruise experience.With the expectation that the high passenger growth in the last decade will continue, the industry actively seeks new destinations and often will contribute to the development of a new port facility seeking calls from cruise vessels.

One example of this is a new port of call in Mexico. Construction of that facility will be a joint venture between the owner of a Mexican nature park and a cruise line, and when constructed will be able to handle four 100,000 tonne ships simultaneously.The terminal design will feature Mayan motif relating to the local culture. An additional example is a recent investment by the industry in a Bahamian shipyard that will contribute skilled jobs into the local economy.

ICCL cruise line members demonstrate a commitment to environmental excellence that is embodied through their social responsibility. The industry promotes good stewardship of the marine environment through varying internal and external initiatives.They involve their crew members in reducing the number, volume and composition of chemicals used on ships and work with them to identify opportunities to reduce, reuse and recycle whenever possible.

Cruise guests are educated on the importance of using waste containers to ensure discarded items do not go over the side. Not only is recycling a part of the ships' day-to-day operating procedures, but passengers are also encouraged to assist in the effort by using special recycling bins located around the ships. The industry favours contracting with vendors, suppliers and service providers who have made their own commitment to similar standards for safety and health, as well as continuous improvement.

Cruise lines generally donate to charitable causes throughout the world, including their local home ports and major ports of call.The following examples are just a brief overview of cruise line efforts to promote local environmental stewardship. In 2001, FCCA cruise line members partnered with St. Lucia, and Nassau, (Bahamas), to conduct the annual FCCA Caribbean Environmental Awareness Project. As part of their ongoing effort to spread environmental awareness, this project is staged every year throughout the Caribbean. In Nassau, more than 100 crew members teamed up, and were divided up into teams and given various tasks to beautify a section of Lighthouse Beach as follows:

— removing sand that had been blown on to the walkway from past hurricanes,

— re-distributing the sand over the rocks that had been exposed,

— development of a native tree garden with rock formations,
— white-washing the exterior of the beach facilities,
— painting of concession stands for local vendors,
— construction of an obstacle course and play area for children.

Grants have been awarded to the Centre for Marine Conservation and the World Wildlife Fund, the Alaska SeaLife Centre, Bahamas Reef Environment Educational Foundation, National Audubon Society and Earthwatch Institute. Steward Council launched in March 2000 a public awareness campaign in the United States, Europe and Australia to promote long-term sustainable fishing, using the power of consumers and the certification of fisheries. Through global use of the Marine Steward Council logo, seafood companies and consumers will be encouraged to purchase fish only from those certified with environmentally responsible practices.

Opportunities for Employment

Cruise industry employment provides substantial opportunities for employees from developing nations. Approximately 85% to 90% of ICCL cruise industry employees are hired from the international workforce. Many of these employees are from developing nations where employment is often limited and difficult in terms of either opportunity or stability.Through cruise line employment, these men and women not only become economically independent, but in many cases direct a portion of their income back to their country of origin through contributions to family members.This way, the cruise industry not only provides a high level of economic opportunity for those who are employed, but also helps sustain these families in their home countries and feeds funds into local economies.

Moreover, a growing number of women across the globe are finding economic opportunities within the cruise industry.The devastating effects of poverty are particularly severe on women in nations struggling with a weak economy and oppressive social and cultural factors beyond their control.Women are relegated to either very low-paying wages or non-employment.Those women who are employed by the cruise industry enjoy personal autonomy from a sustained income that is not matched in their own country.

In essence, the cruise industry has provided opportunity for women to achieve increased economic, social and cultural equality. Another aspect of the benefits gained through cruise ship employment lies in the value of the skills acquired in the course of work aboard a ship.Training in new technologies, cross-cultural awareness, certification in management practices and hands-on experience brings added benefits to the employee.There are comprehensive education and training programmes in place for crew members, primarily to ensure that there are not inadvertent violations of environmental policies, and to heighten sensitivities to environmental issues.

When they return to their country of origin, the employees utilise their experiences, training and resources for the benefit of the local economy and fellow nationals.They also develop a sense of empowerment and leadership that comes from pride in position, economic autonomy and the development of contacts with nationals of other countries. The working and living environment that the employee enjoys is clean, safe and controlled by international and United States laws. Room, board and medical care are provided by the industry, as well as the ability to experience international travel.The standard of medical care is excellent and usually far exceeds that of their country of origin.

Environmental Impact

ICCL member cruise lines are dedicated to preserving the marine environment, and the pristine condition of the waters upon which their vessels sail, and demonstrate this by a reduction of waste by over 50% over the past decade.As an industry that is based on carrying passengers to locations where they can experience and enjoy the beauties provided by nature or human achievements, ICCL members recognise that even a perception that the industry is not meeting relevant international and local environmental standards around the world is damaging to their image and therefore their business prospects.

ICCL members have made a substantial investment in new building with over 32 ships scheduled for delivery between 2001 to 2005. With a capital cost of USD12 billion, the industry's investment in the future is substantial. With these realities in mind, ICCL member cruise lines have established standards regarding environmental practices and ship safety. In the past, initiatives such as ICCL's Waste Management Practices and Procedures were strictly voluntary guidelines. The member lines of ICCL have agreed to adhere to these as standards, thus demonstrating the commitment of its members to protecting the safety and health of people on-board cruise ships, as well as the marine environment. ICCL members believe that these self-imposed voluntary industry standards meet or exceed all requirements of the law wherever ICCL ships operate throughout the world.

Cruise Industry Waste Management

Practices and Procedures document was unanimously adopted by ICCL membership in June 2001, as an attachment to ICCL Mandatory Environmental Standard.The procedures enumerated in this document have been incorporated into all ICCL member lines' operating policies using as a vehicle, the requirements of the International Safety Management Code (ISM), which is a mandatory chapter of SOLAS.This is the first time an association of international vessel operators has adopted mandatory waste management practices and procedures. Compliance with this comprehensive environmental standard is now a condition of ICCL membership.

The goal of this initiative is to embrace the most advanced technology and procedures in order to establish a leadership position in environmental compliance and reduce the industry's environmental impact.This decision has far-reaching implications in sectors of the world where marine and shore environments are intricately linked to the social, commercial and economic status of its inhabitants. The goals and objectives are set by the Environmental Committee of ICCL, which is comprised of representatives from all 16 member cruise lines.As a sign of their commitment, ICCL members continuously seek out and test new environmental and safety technologies. In keeping with this commitment, numerous ICCL members have invested millions of dollars to purchase and field test new advanced technology in graywater and blackwater (sewage) treatment.

These advanced treatment systems, when fully developed and proven, are expected to remove sediments and impurities from shipboard waste water streams to the point that the output is essentially clean water.This clean water may then be reused or discharged without fear of any environmental impact. Additionally, ICCL member lines are investigating new technologies for dry-cleaning operations, photo processing, and digital imaging in order to reduce the production of hazardous waste. New on-board incineration systems are being investigated to improve the efficiency and cleanliness of on-board disposal of waste that cannot be recycled or reused. The industry has also developed relationships with state and local officials in various communities on which it calls to establish co-operative relationships and to demonstrate its commitment to solving environmental challenges.

For example, in Alaska, ICCL members have paid for waste water and air monitoring and have committed to discharging wastewater only when a vessel is underway at a speed of at least six knots, and away from port. ICCL members are committed to continuous improvement.Through this commitment, ICCL members have endorsed policy goals based upon the following fundamental principles:

— full compliance with applicable international laws and regulations;
— maintaining co-operative relationships with the regulatory community in the United States and internationally;
— designing, constructing and operating vessels so as to minimise their impact on the environment;
— embracing new technology;
— conserving resources through purchasing strategies and product management;
— minimising waste generated and maximising reuse and recycling;
— optimising energy efficiency through conservation and management;
— managing water discharges;
— educating staff, guests and the community.

The mechanism for accountability is established by placing the Mandatory Standards into each company and ship's Safety Management System (SMS).The requirement for a SMS is detailed in the ISM Code, which was mentioned previously. Additionally, the ISM Code requires annual internal audits of the SMS, as well as biannual third party audits conducted by a recognised auditor named by the vessel's flag state as acceptable for performing this task.The results of compliance audits for each vessel are archived and may be made available to appropriate enforcement entities upon request.

Practices and Procedures document also forms the basis for a memorandum of understanding (MOU) between the State of Florida and the Florida Caribbean Cruise Association (FCCA) that was signed 6 December 2001. It has been utilised in discussions with federal agencies such as the United States Coast Guard and the United States EPA, as well as the Alaska Department of Environmental Conservation (DEC) and legislators in Washington, Alaska and California.

It is important to the industry to establish partnerships with governments.The ICCL's success has been based on continuing partnerships with government agencies and local communities. ICCL members have invested a large amount of time and resources to initiating and continuing the partnership with United States Coast Guard, joint environmental studies with Florida Environmental protection Agency (EPA) and MOU with the Florida Department of Environmental protection (DEP) in order to contribute to the objective of sustainable tourism development.

In response to a petition from a number of environmental groups, United States EPA developed an action plan to evaluate cruise ship wastewater discharges as well as the industry's environmental operating practices. Public meetings were held in Juneau, (Alaska), Los Angeles, (California) and Miami, (Florida) as a part of EPA's evaluation process. As a cooperative partnership issue, the United States Coast Guard together with ICCL, co-hosted a two-day workshop for United States EPA, other federal officials, cruise industry segments and public environmental advocacy groups. This forum focused on the practical application of the international regulatory regime and other aspects of environmental management practices adopted by

ICCL vessel operators. In August 2001, United States EPA sampled waste water discharges from cruise ships and will utilise this research to determine dispersion patterns and, in turn, environmental impacts of cruise ship waste water discharges. This effort is being conducted with the full support and co-operation of ICCL members.

ICCL welcomes the opportunity to demonstrate global adherence to these best practices, and responsibility to environmental preservation. ICCL knows of no other segment of maritime industry that will be willing or able to meet these types of standards. Indeed, ICCL is raising the bar for global environmental performance in maritime industry.

Health and Safety

In the 1970s, because of several gastrointestinal illness outbreaks on cruise vessels, the United States Centre for Disease Control (CDC) established the Vessel Sanitation Programme (VSP) as a co-operative activity with the cruise ship industry.The programme assists the cruise ship industry in fulfilling its responsibility for developing and implementing comprehensive sanitation programmes, in order to minimise the risk for gastro-intestinal diseases. ICCL has embraced this programme to ensure health and safety on-board cruise ships.

Health and safety is built into every aspect of a cruise ship beginning at the vessel's design stage. CDC, in partnership with the cruise industry and the shipyards, developed construction guidelines for the various components of the vessel's facilities that are related to public health.These include food storage areas, refrigerators and freezers, food preparation service and serving areas, water bunkering, storage, disinfecting, and distribution systems, the construction of pools and spas, and many other aspects of ship construction.

Currently, over 140 cruise ships participate in the programme.The inspections are conducted by Environmental Health Officers (EHO) of the United States VSP, and take place only in United States ports.The inspection focuses on the following: the ship's water supply, spas and pools, potential for food or water contamination, practices and personal hygiene of employees, general cleanliness and physical condition of the ship, and the environmental and public health practices training programmes.

Since the programme began, the number of disease illness outbreaks on ships has declined significantly despite substantial growth in the number of ships sailing and the number of passengers carried.

Cruise ship companies frequently ask the VSP staff to help them improve their on-board sanitation efforts. Since December 1989,VSP staff has offered sanitation seminars four times each year for shipboard personnel.These seminars bridge the communication gap between government regulators and shipboard personnel by explaining recommended standards, emphasising the reasons for them, and discussing how to comply with them.Topics covered are: the storage, distribution, protection and disinfecting of a ship's water supply, protection of food during storage, preparation, cooking, and service, employee practices and personal hygiene, general cleanliness, facility repair, vector control, and potential for contamination of food and water. This programme is also a global training environment for the shipboard employees from developing nations.

Education, hands-on training and practical application in sanitation and the reduction of the risk of disease are skill sets that are applicable in their home countries.This training is often not available in the developing world or there are constraints due to the lack of trained professionals available. Often cruise ship staff attain leadership status in their communities as a direct result of being exposed to advanced training and practical experience opportunities.

Over the past two decades, an estimated 60 million passengers enjoyed a cruise vacation. During this period, not one passenger death due to a marine incident (such as a fire, collision, or grounding) occurred on any ICCL vessel operating from a United States port. This enviable safety record is the direct result of the important focus that is placed in this area. Of course, the cruise industry cannot be complacent; ICCL constantly investigates ways to improve its performance.

This excellent safety record demonstrates ICCL members' commitment to safety. In 1996, the United States Coast Guard published a comprehensive cruise ship safety study, which concluded that the industry was one of the safest modes of transportation available and that international safety initiatives coming into force would further improve its safety record. As reported by this task force, many SOLAS requirements 'are now significantly more stringent than United States regulations.'This is especially true with regard to fire protection. No other form of transportation (bus, train, or aeroplane) can claim to be as safe as a vacation cruise or provide as extensive fire emergency and life support systems.

If a cruise ship sails from a United States port, the United States Coast Guard has conducted an in-depth examination of that ship for safety.The United States Coast Guard reviews the ship plans for compliance with construction requirements and then visits the vessel while under construction to assure it is properly built.The United States Coast Guard also verifies the adequacy of crew training through observation of drills, examination of documentation, and interviews with officers and crew.

To assure compliance with safety regulations, the United States Coast Guard exercises portstate control authority over foreign flag cruise ships operating from

United States ports. Other maritime agencies exercise port-state control under similar programmes in the ports where they have jurisdiction.The United States Coast Guard, in accordance with its Control Verification Examination (CVE) programme, conducts quarterly inspections on all vessels embarking passengers at United States ports. The examinations focus on fire safety systems and life saving equipment and their safety and environmental protection items. Additionally, the United States Coast Guard witnesses fire and abandon ship drills to ensure crew proficiency.The average response time for an on-board emergency is within a matter of minutes—fire teams and trained emergency and medical crews are always only a few hundred feet away.

The formalised partnership with the United States Coast Guard has resulted in meetings on a regular basis both at the executive and technical levels to discuss emerging safety issues and recent passenger vessel initiatives adopted or under consideration at IMO.The partnership has planned and co-ordinated joint emergency preparedness exercises to ensure the effectiveness of response capabilities, has worked on methods to identify lessons learned from past marine casualties, and has instituted crew training policies in response to STCW.

ICCL believes this partnership is a productive way to exchange information on the operational impacts of proposed policies as well as identification of resources required to respond to various types of vessel emergencies.The partnership between ICCL and the United States Coast Guard has been a factor in the establishment of industry standards for lifejackets in excess of international requirements, infant personal flotation devices, and helicopter pick-up areas.

Security of Passenger

The highest priority of the cruise industry is to provide a

safe and secure vacation experience for our passengers.The cruise industry takes any and all cases of reported crimes on-board our ships seriously. Every person on-board a cruise ship, from the captain to the cleaning staff and all guests, is placed on an official manifest. Passengers and crew may embark or disembark only after passing through security. Access is strictly limited to documented employees and fare-paying passengers. Most importantly, since 11 September 2001, the cruise industry has heightened its security measures both on and off the vessel in order to provide the most secure environment for its passengers and crew.

Even though a cruise ship is inherently secure because it is a controlled environment with limited access, immediately following the terrorist attacks all ICCL members implemented Security Level III, even before the United States Coast Guard (USCG) ordered it. Security Level III is the highest level of security set by Coast Guard Passenger Vessel Security regulations. At United States cruise terminals, passenger vessel security measures include passenger screening procedures similar to those found at airports.This includes 100% screening of all passenger baggage, carry-on luggage, ship stores and cargo, and also includes higher levels of screening of passenger identification. Official passenger lists are carefully reviewed and proper identification is ensured before anyone is allowed to board the vessel.

Coast Guard regulations implemented in 1996 require ship operators to submit Comprehensive Security Plans to the USCG for review and acceptance.These regulations address both passenger ship and passenger terminal security and outline methods to deter unlawful activities on-board. All ICCL member lines have submitted security plans that have been accepted by USCG and these plans are audited annually. Since 1998, ICCL and its member operators have been members of the United States

Interagency Task Force on Passenger Vessel Security.This group meets every 60 days to discuss emerging security issues, receive updated threat information, and address specific security concerns. Since 11 September 2001, ICCL Security and Operations Committee members have efficiently communicated and resolved problems in daily conference calls with all of the appropriate federal agencies.This information exchange has proven to be valuable both to our member lines and the federal agencies involved as we mutually address matters impacting both ship operations and security.

Cruise lines operate within a very strict legal framework that gives international, federal and state authorities the right to investigate crimes on-board cruise ships. Unlike most instances of crime ashore, the United States Federal Bureau of Investigation (FBI) has the authority to investigate alleged crimes in international waters when an American is involved. In July 1999, ICCL executives announced an industrywide position regarding the reporting of crimes committed on-board cruise ships.

Incidents of criminal conduct are extremely low in comparison to similar incidents reported ashore. FBI and United States Census Bureau statistics indicate that the numbers of reported crimes in United States communities are at least 20 times greater than the number of reported shipboard assaults per capita.This level of security is carried on ICCL's ships as they travel around the world and visit the ports of many countries.

The cruise industry has taken a proactive role in addressing the provision of shipboard medical care. Over five years ago, members of ICCL began work on development of industry-wide guidelines for the medical facilities, staffing, equipment and procedures utilised on-board passenger vessels.Then, in 1996 it issued guidelines that represented the work of a group of experienced medical physicians and other medical experts knowledgeable about the unique needs and limitations of shipboard medical care. During this effort, ICCL worked in conjunction with the American College of Emergency Physicians (ACEP), the national association representing over 20,000 practising emergency and other physicians in the United States and abroad.

ACEP's Section of Cruise Ship and Maritime Medicine are specifically dedicated to training, education and research in the advancement of shipboard medical care. Medical Facilities Guidelines are intended to foster the following goals to provide reasonable emergency medical care for passengers and crew on-board cruise vessels, to stabilise patients and/or initiate reasonable diagnostic and therapeutic intervention, and to facilitate the evacuation of seriously ill or injured patients when deemed necessary by a shipboard physician.

Subsequent to the passage of the Americans with Disabilities Act (ADA), the Passenger Vessel Access Advisory Committee (PVAAC) was empanelled by the United States Architectural and Transportation Barrier Compliance Board to make recommendations for the development of regulations that would improve accessibility for persons with disabilities on-board passenger-carrying vessels ICCL participated in all discussions.The PVAAC report was presented to the board in Miami on 17 November 2000.

In the meantime, ICCL cruise members have included new and innovative ideas and technologies in their newly constructed ships and have, in most instances, modified older ships to provide improved access to all public spaces for guests with many different types of disabilities - not just the mobility impaired. All this has been done at the initiative of the cruise vessel operators without detailed regulation.

The international cruise industry has a remarkable story of success and achievement in a number of sectors, not the least of which has been our safety record, particularly for the 16 cruise line members of ICCL.This success could only have been achieved through the teamwork with industry partners and the innovation, energy and devotion of many very talented individuals. Moreover, because there is a mutual interdependence between the cruise line industry and the countries visited by its ships, there is a bright future. As the industry grows, so will the issues and challenges that it faces.

Issues that the industry will be focusing on in the future include safety, environmental management, and continued product enhancements. As the ships become more complex, and the locations visited become more distant, the sophistication of cruising operations will grow exponentially.Through private-public sector relationships, solutions can be devised for all issues and challenges.As global leaders in the maritime industry, the members of ICCL will always be at the cutting edge in the utilisation of new technologies. As passenger demand increases and the cruise industry continues to grow, ICCL and its member lines will continue to participate in the development of new IMO safety initiatives that govern the operation of cruise vessels worldwide.

Over the past several years, IMO has adopted several new international regulations that significantly enhance passenger vessel safety.These comprehensive IMO regulations established stringent new standards that require significant fire safety upgrades for new and existing vessels, adopted advanced crew safety training requirements, and required all vessels to implement a specified safety management system that delineates crew responsibilities and establishes mandatory codes of practice.These are internationally mandated by the United States government; both flag-state and port-state authorities closely monitor standards, and treaties are adopted throughout the world.

Future Goals and Challenges

To achieve the goals and challenges set for the travel and tourism industry as it continues to grow throughout the coming decades, will require a strong and co-operative partnership between government departments, national tourism authorities, international and national trade associations, trade unions and the travel and tourism private sector. All stakeholders now need to share the responsibility for travel and tourism's future and need to deliver the following to ensure its sustainability:

Governments need to:

a) integrate travel and tourism policy, especially the environment, into broader government policies;

b) set up realistic capacities within sustainability frameworks, which have been set in consultation with industry and other stakeholders;

c) create incentives for the travel and tourism industry backed up where necessary by effective regulation;

d) be committed to the controlled expansion, where appropriate, of infrastructure;

e) apply environmental taxes fairly and nondiscriminatorily, where needed.They should be carefully thought out to minimise their impact on economic development, and revenues should be allocated to travel- and tourism-associated environment improvement programmes;

f) set up mechanisms to support SMEs in the adoption of sustainable good practice;

g) design policies creating incentives for corporate social responsibility in tourism, favouring a sensitive and engaging approach towards the local communities at the destinations, especially in the developing countries.

Public-private partnerships need to:

a) plan and develop infrastructure with a long-term view and within a reference framework based on Agenda 21;

b) implement indicators and environmental impact assessment tools to enable successful and effective local management and appropriate development;

c) agree on common standards and tools to enable the measurement of progress towards achieving sustainable development;

d) fund and develop contemporary research into sustainable tourism.

Issues requiring attention include design, carrying capacity, tour operator activities, environmental reporting, and auditing and environmental impact assessments, socio-economic sustainability of the tourism businesses.

International bodies need to:

a) co-ordinate environmental action to be undertaken by all sectors of the travel and tourism industry, at an international level;

b) review existing voluntary initiatives to improve the quality of reporting, their transparency and credibility, and the assessment of their contribution to sustainability;

c) ensure that all funding, from international, national and local funding bodies, should be dependent on sound environmental practice;

d) encourage and support multi-stakeholder projects aiming for sustainable tourism development;

e) set up mechanisms to support the adoption of sustainable good practices by SMEs.

Private sector companies need to:

a) commit to place sustainable development issues at the core of the management structure;

b) develop and more widely apply certification criteria to industry initiatives;

c) innovate processes and applications through new technology;

d) make a commitment to the education and environmental training of staff;

e) encourage corporate citizenship as the standard for private sector companies;

f) be willing to engage in multi-stakeholder dialogue.

2

Organisation of Loadging

The structure of a lodging business must be consistent with its strategy.Managers give structure to a hotel and lodging through job specialization, organization, and establishment of patterns of authority and span of control. Separating departments by function is the most common method of organising a lodging business. In a very small lodging business, the owner can supervise each department. However, as the lodging business increases in size, it is most effective to create managerial positions within departments.

As their facilities grow in size, lodging managers are faced with the need to group certain jobs in order to ensure efficient coordination and control of activities. These job groupings are usually called departments. In general, departments might be grouped as front of the house (those departments in which employees have guest contact, such as front desk), and back of the house (where employees have little guest contact, such as accounting).

Responsibilities of Rooms Department

Rooms department includes reservations, the front office, housekeeping, and telephone or PBX. In smaller full-service hotels, security and engineering might also be included in the rooms department. Responsibilities of the rooms department include reservations, guest reception, room assignment, tracking the status of rooms, prompt forwarding of mail and phone messages, security, housekeeping of guest rooms and public spaces such as lobbies, and answering guests' questions. To perform these many duties effectively, the rooms department may be divided into a number of specialized subunits. To complicate matters, in many instances these subunits are also referred to as departments.

The front office is one of the most important departments in a hotel, as it often offers the only contact between guests and staff. A hotel's front office is where guests are greeted when they arrive, where they are registered and assigned to a room, and where they check out. Usually, the telephone operator, other guest communications functions, and the bell staff or those employees responsible for delivering luggage and messages and attending to special guest requests also fall under the front office umbrella. The reservations department takes and tracks the hotel's future bookings.

The housekeeping department is responsible for cleaning guest rooms and public spaces. Because of their specialized nature, the security and engineering departments are discussed in separate sections. A great deal of interdependence exists among the subunits of the rooms department. For example, reservations must inform the front office of the number of presold rooms each day to ensure that a current inventory of salable rooms is always available. On the other hand, the front office must let reservations know whenever walk-in guests (those who do not have reservations) register. A similar level of cooperation is required between the front office and housekeeping. When a guest checks out, the front office must inform housekeeping so that the room may be cleaned. Once a room is cleaned, housekeeping must inform the front office so that the room may be sold. Certain tasks within the rooms department must occur in a specific order.

For example, housekeeping cannot properly provision a guest room if the laundry does not supply enough clean towels or bed sheets. Engineering cannot replace a defective light switch in a guest room if housekeeping does not report the problem. Effective management of this busy department calls for standardized plans, procedures, schedules, and deadlines, as well as frequent direct communication between the executives who manage the key operating units of the rooms department.

Security: The hotel and lodging business is vulnerable to security and safety problems. Problems can be created by guests, employees, or intruders. Security breaches can result in embezzlement, theft, arson, robbery, and even terrorism. Depending on the size of a hotel or a lodging establishment, the security function may be handled by a fully staffed department on site, contracted to an outside security company, or assigned to designated staff members or on-premises supervisory percsonnel in the rooms department. In a larger, full-service hotel, the director of security may report directly to the general manager. In smaller hotels, the security function might become a task of the rooms department.

Engineering: Engineering department's responsibilities include preventive maintenance; repair; replacement; improvement and modification to furniture, fixtures, and equipment (FFE); and ensuring uninterrupted provision of utilities (gas, electricity, water).Preventive maintenance involves routine checks and inspection of the key components of all equipment. Maintenance of recreational facilities may be part of the engineering department's responsibilities. In particular, swimming pools require extensive maintenance to ensure proper filtration and to prevent the accumulation of algae and other conditions unsuitable for swimming. Prompt repair minimizes loss of productivity in other hotel operating departments and inconvenience to hotel guests.

When a particular FFE has reached the end of its useful life and repair is no longer cost-effective, replacement is indicated. Improvement projects enhance the existing operation or reduce operating costs of the facility. Modification projects alter the existing operation to accommodate one or more new functions. One hotel might have a large engineering staff that includes plumbers, carpenters, painters, electricians, and other technicians. Another might have maintenance personnel who have general knowledge and understanding of the hotel's operations but rely on outside contractors for specialized jobs. In larger, full-service hotels, engineering may be a separate department, with a director who reports directly to the resident manager.

Food and Beverage Department: The primary function of the food and beverage department is to provide food and drink to a hotel's guests. In earlier times, when an inn had a single dining room that could hold a limited number of guests, this was a fairly simple task. Today, however, providing food and drink is much more complicated. A large hotel might well have a coffee shop, a gourmet restaurant, a poolside snack bar, room service, two banquet halls, and ten function rooms where food and beverages are served. It might also have a lounge, a nightclub, and a lobby bar.

On a busy day (or night), it's quite likely that functions will be booked in many outlets at the same time. In addition, some outlets may have multiple events scheduled for a single day. As you can see, there is great diversity in the types of activities performed by a food and beverage department, requiring a significant variety of skills on the part of its workers. Because of the diversity of services provided, the food and beverage department is typically split into subunits. The executive chef, a person of considerable importance and authority in any full-service hotel, runs the food production, or kitchen, department. A variety of culinary specialists who are responsible for different aspects of food preparation report to the executive chef.

The actual serving of food in a large hotel's restaurants is usually the responsibility of a separate department, headed by the assistant food and beverage director. The food service department is composed of the individual restaurant and outlet managers, maitre d's, waiters, waitresses, and bus help. Because of their special duties and concerns, many large hotels have a separate subunit that is responsible only for room service. Because of the high value and profit margins associated with the sale of alcoholic beverages, some hotels have a separate department that assumes responsibility for all outlets where alcoholic beverages are sold. The person responsible for this department is the beverage manager. Most full-service hotels also do a considerable convention and catering business. The typical convention uses small function rooms for meetings and larger rooms for general sessions, trade shows, exhibits, and banquets.

As a hotel or lodging business increases the use of its facilities for conventions and meetings, it may form a separate convention services department. The convention services department and its personnel are introduced to the client, a meeting planner, or an association executive by the marketing and sales department. The convention services department then handles all of the client's meeting and catering requirements. Individually catered events include parties, wedding receptions, business meetings, and other functions held by groups.

To provide for the unique needs of these types of customers, hotels often organise separate catering and convention departments. Depending on the size of the hotel, the job of cleaning the food and beverage outlets themselves as well as of washing pots and pans, dishes, glasses, and utensils is often delegated to a subunit known as the stewarding department. It is only through continuous cooperation and coordination that a hotel's food service function can be carried out effectively.

A guest who is dining in a hotel restaurant requires the joint efforts of the kitchen, food service, beverage, and stewarding departments. A convention banquet cannot be held without the efforts of the convention and catering department along with the food production, beverage, and stewarding departments. The sequence of events and cooperation required among the food and beverage staff is even more important than in the rooms department, thus increasing the importance of communication between managers and employees alike. Another challenge faced by management is the diversity of the employees in the food and beverage department; the dishwasher in the stewarding department is at a dramatically different level than the sous chef in the kitchen.

Marketing and Sales Department: The primary responsibility of the sales managers who make up the marketing and sales department is sales, or the selling of the hotel facilities and services to individuals and groups. Sales managers sell rooms, food, and beverages to potential clients through advertising, attendance at association and conference meetings, and direct contacts. The marketing and sales department is also removed from most of the day-to-day operational problems faced by other departments. The division of work among the sales managers is based on the type of customers a hotel is attempting to attract. Individual sales managers often specialize in corporate accounts, conventions, or tour and travel markets. Sales managers' accounts are sometimes subdivided along geographical lines into regional or national accounts.

Human Resource Department : The human resources department serves no customers, books no business, and prepares no meals, yet it plays a vital role in a hotel's efficient operation. The three functions of the human resources department are

a) employee recruitment,

b) benefits administration, and

c) training.

The director of human resources is also expected to be an expert on federal and state labor laws and to advise managers in other departments on these topics. The human resources department's major challenge is in its interactions with other hotel departments. Although the human resources department recruits, interviews, and screens prospective employees, the final hiring decision rests within the department in which the potential employee will be working. The same is true of promotion and disciplinary decisions; the human resources department's input is, in most cases, limited to advice and interpretation of legal questions. The human resources department's effectiveness depends on its manager's ability to form effective working relationships with managers of other departments.

Accounting Department: The accounting department's traditional role is recording financial transactions, preparing and interpreting financial statements, and providing the managers of other departments with timely reports of operating results (line functions). The accounting department combines staff functions and line functions, or those functions directly responsible for servicing guests. Other responsibilities, carried out by the assistant controller for finance, include payroll preparation, accounts receivable, and accounts payable (staff functions).

Another dimension of the accounting department's responsibilities deals with various aspects of hotel operations, cost accounting, and cost control throughout the hotel. The two areas of central concern to the accounting department are rooms and food and beverage. The accounting department's front office cashier is responsible for tracking all charges to guest accounts. At the close of each business day, which varies by hotel but typically occurs at midnight or after the bulk of guests' transactions have been completed (i.e., check-in, restaurant charges, retail charges, etc.), the night auditor is responsible for reconciling all guest bills with the charges from the various hotel departments.

Although the front office cashier and the night auditor physically work at the front desk and, in the case of the cashier, have direct contact with guests, they are members of the accounting department and report to the assistant controller of operations. The food and beverage department may be responsible for food preparation and service, but the accounting department is responsible for collecting revenues. The food and beverage controller and the food and beverage cashiers keep track of both the revenues and expenses of the food and beverage department.

The food and beverage controller's job is to verify the accuracy and reasonableness of all food and beverage revenues. In addition to tracking and preparing daily reports on the costs of the food and beverages used in the hotel, in many cases the accounting department is also responsible for purchasing and storeroom operations. Finally, the director of systems is responsible for designing the accounting and control systems used throughout the hotel. As you can see, the accounting department is anything but a passive staff unit contending with routine recordkeeping.

The accounting department is also responsible for collecting and reporting most of a hotel's operational and financial statistics, which provide important data for decision making and budget preparation purposes. The head of the accounting department may report not only to the hotel's general manager but also to the hotel chain's financial vice president or to the hotel's owner. The reason for this dual responsibility and reporting relationship is to afford the hotel corporation an independent verification of the financial and operating results of the hotel.

General Manager: Hotel's general manager (GM) is responsi-ble for defining and interpreting the policies established by top management. The general manager serves as a liaison to the hotel's owner or corporate parent, sets (or communicates) the overall strategic course of the hotel, sets hotel-wide goals, coordinates activities between departments, and arbitrates interdepartmental disputes. It is common practice in a large, full-service hotel for a director of public relations to report directly to the GM. The GM also has corporate-level responsibilities, participates on civic boards and committees, and engages in industry-related activities such as serving on the local tourism commission or hotel-motel association.

In addition to possessing a high level of technical skill (i.e., a thorough understanding of each operating department in the hotel), the general manager must also be decisive, analytical, and skilled with both computers and people. He or she must be able to see the big picture and how all of the parts of the hotel fit into the overall organisation.

Resident Manager: An executive may be promoted to relieve the general manager of some operational duties. This is often accomplished by elevating the duties and responsibilities of one particular department head without relieving that person of regular departmental duties. The title of this position is usually resident manager. It is quite common (and logical) for the general manager to select the manager of the rooms department to be resident manager. Responsibilities of the resident manager include serving as acting GM in the GM's absence, representing the GM on interdepartmental hotel committees, and taking responsibility for important special projects such as major hotel renovations, VIP guests, and operating reports that require in-depth analysis for the regional or corporate offices.

Pattorns of Authority

Defined simply, authority is the organisationally sanctioned right to make a decision. Authority can be distributed throughout an organisation or held in the hands of a few select employees. The delegation of authority creates a chain of command, the formal channel that defines the lines of authority from the top to the bottom of an organisation. The chain of command specifies a clear reporting relationship for each person in the organisation and should be followed in both downward and upward communication. Following the chain of command enables each new employee, no matter what his or her position, to know exactly for whom and to whom he or she is responsible. When designing an organisational structure, managers must consider the distribution of authority.

Decentralization is the process of distributing authority throughout an organisation. In a decentralized organisation, an organisation member has the right to make a decision without obtaining approval from a higher-level manager. Centralization is the retention of decision-making authority by a high-level manager. Traditionally, hotel and lodging management has been very centralized, probably due to its roots in small, owner-operated lodging. In recent years, as the hotel and lodging industry has expanded, decentralization has become a more frequent style of operation.

Decentralization has several advantages. Managers are encouraged to develop decision-making skills, which help them advance in their careers. The autonomy afforded by this style of operation also increases job satisfaction and motivation. When employees are encouraged to perform well, the profitability of the organisation increases. Many hotel and lodging organisations have begun to empower employees and supervisors to make decisions that typically have been made by managers. One example that we have already discussed is the use of the quality circle.

For example, if a front desk agent determines that a guest's bill is incorrect, in a decentralized organisation the agent has the power to make the correction immediately. If that same front desk agent determines that a guest's stay has been unsatisfactory, he or she has the power to reduce the guest's bill by an amount previ- ously specified by management. Additional challenges, control of the process, and quality assessment become part of everyone's job, and each employee is given the authority to take positive actions that will lead to high quality and improved performance.

Span of Control

It refers to the number of people who report to one manager or supervisor. A wide span of control results in a flat organisation that is, a large number of employees reporting to one supervisor. A narrow span of control results in a tall organisation, in which a small number of employees report to a supervisor, necessitating a larger number of supervisors. No formula exists for determining the ideal span of control. The following factors determine the most appropriate span of control:

a) task similarity,
b) training and professionalism,
c) task certainty,
d) frequency of interaction,
e) task integration, and
f) physical dispersion.

When a large number of employees perform similar tasks, the span of control can be increased. When the employees perform very different tasks, the supervisor must give each subordinate more individual attention in order to keep in touch with the different types of tasks; this requires a narrower span of control. For example, the rooms department manager might easily manage the front desk agents and housekeepers until the brand standards for check-in or checkout of a guest increase in complexity and the standards for the various types of rooms and their cleaning procedure increase in detail. At this time, the rooms department manager's span of control must be narrowed.

The better trained and more skilled a subordinate is, the less supervision is required. For example, a front desk agent might require a higher level of training and skill than a room service waiter. Thus, a front desk supervisor can supervise more employees (wider span of control) than the room service supervisor (narrower span of control). Task certainty refers to the predictability of a task. Routine tasks allow management to devise standard procedures for subordinates to follow, minimizing questions about the job and widening the span of control. On the other hand, close supervision is called for when tasks are ambiguous and uncertainty is great. For example, the task of checking a guest in or out of the hotel can be documented and standard procedures can be created, so the front desk manager can have a rel-atively wide span of control over the front desk agents.

However, because of the diversity of customers the sales manager encounters, the tasks of a hotel sales manager are less certain. The director of sales is responsible for coaching the sales managers, observing sales calls, and ensuring deal closings; these tasks require a hands-on approach that limits the number of employees the director of sales can handle, narrowing the span of control. If the supervisor-subordinate relationship requires frequent interaction, the span of control must be narrow. If interaction is infrequent, the span of control can be wide. For example, the hotel controller must review regularly the status of collections and payments with staff.

In contrast, the frequency of interaction between the chief engineer and his or her subordinates is directed by written work orders in most circumstances and thus requires less direct communication, enabling a wider span of control. If the supervisor must integrate and coordinate the tasks of subordinates, the span of control narrows. For example, in the production of a meal for one table of four guests with different appetizers, salads, and entrées, the chef must have a narrow span of control to ensure that each component of the meal is assembled correctly and delivered to service personnel on a timely basis. The span of control of the executive housekeeper can be much wider because the procedure for cleaning and preparing each guest room is similar, if not exactly the same, for every room.

Physical dispersion refers to the distribution of employees within the lodging establishment. For example, if the executive housekeeper has guest room attendants on 20 floors in two buildings and the front desk manager has all front desk agents located in one place, the span of control would narrow for the executive housekeeper and widen for the front desk manager. The ideal number of people that one person can supervise depends on a variety of factors. Consistent with trends in organisational structure such as teams, quality circles, and employee empowerment, many hotel and lodging organisations are widening their span of control. The objective behind these trends is to develop a flatter, more responsive organisational structure in which employees can make decisions without going through several levels of management.

Functional Organisation

The most important strength of a functional organisational design is efficiency. The performance of common tasks allows for work specialization, which increases overall productivity. Workers develop specialized skills and knowledge more rapidly. Training is easier because of the similarity of tasks and the resulting opportunities for inexperienced workers to learn from experienced workers. This helps new employees quickly learn the kinds of behavior that lead to success and promotion. Coordination of activities within functional departments is easier than in more broadly based organisations.

A functional organisation fosters efficiency, teamwork, and coordination of activities within individual units. However, the functional organisation's most important strength is also the source of its great-est shortcoming. The success of a hotel as a business is measured by its overall performance and not by the performance of any one department. A hotel with spotless guest rooms will not be successful if guests' front desk experiences are not up to par.

Even if guests' dining experiences are superb, the hotel will fall flat on its face if its rooms are dismal. It is sometimes difficult for each department to fully appreciate its role in the overall success of the organisation. It is vital that each department keep in mind the hotel-wide goals of customer service and profitability rather than focus narrowly on its own concerns. Some means must be found to coordinate the activities of functional departments and to set hotel-wide strategies and goals. A hotel's functional organisation demands strong leadership. New initiatives in hotels often require cooperation and coordination between functional departments. New ideas tend to be stillborn if department heads lack a hotel-wide perspective or have difficulty coordinating their activities.

The tendency to concentrate on doing things right often overshadows the organisation's ability to do the right thing.The GM, as the chief executive of the hotel, emerges as the single person capable of providing the overall organisational direction, decision making, coordination, and arbitration needed to make a hotel's functional departments work together effectively. A hotel simply cannot run itself from the departmental level. Thus, the GM must be a strong leader to be effective.

Meeting and Committees

Consider this scenario. If the director of sales increases group bookings without consulting other hotel departments, a disaster is in the making. If the reservations department is not consulted, the sales department might guarantee more rooms to a group than are actually available at a price lower than the reservations department's quarterly goal. If the convention services manager is not consulted, necessary meeting rooms might not be available. If the food and beverage department is not consulted, the group might be sold a banquet that exceeds the hotel's capabilities. If the accounting department is not con- sulted, credit terms might be extended that violate the credit manager's policies. If the front office is not consulted, the group might experience lengthy delays at check-in (groups are usually preassigned rooms and keys).

The executive operating committee (EOC) of a hotel, made up of the general manager and senior executives from each department, is designed to increase the level of coordination between departments. There is no standard membership for this committee, but it usually comprises those executives who report directly to the general manager. The EOC is also responsible for a hotel's major budgetary units, such as the food and beverage and housekeeping units. EOC functions depend on how the hotel GM chooses to use the group, the GM's style, and the structure of other management meetings in the hotel. Typically, the EOC meets weekly, focusing on matters ranging from day-today operational issues (daily function schedules and labor and food cost control) to comparing budgets with actual operating results.

Many hotels increase communications through an elaborate structure of additional committees and meetings, including some or all of the following: operations, staff, sales forecast and marketing, departmental, subdepartmental, credit, safety, energy conservation, and employee meetings. The operations committee comprises the general manager, department heads, front office manager, manager on duty, and representatives from housekeeping, security, engineering, and food and beverage. This committee might meet four or five times per week for 15 to 20 minutes to review upcoming activities and assess the results of previous activities.

The staff committee might include the GM, department heads, and all subdepartment heads who report to the department heads. This committee, which might meet weekly for one or two hours, reviews the prior week's performance, the current week's activities, the next week's plans, and special projects. The staff committee also presents performance awards to employees.

The sales forecast and marketing committee might meet one to four times per month for several hours so the GM and department heads can review room demand for the coming 90 days and devise strategies to increase room nights (and thus bring in more revenue) and to increase average daily rates by up-selling potential guests to higher-rated rooms with perhaps more amenities or services. The departmental committee consists of the department head and his or her subdepartment heads, managers, and supervisors. Meeting once or twice per month for an hour or so, the group reviews departmental issues. Similarly, subdepartment committees meet monthly for about an hour so the subdepartment head, managers, and supervisors can address issues unique to their subdepartment, such as the selection of a new type of floor cleaner by the housekeeping department or a more energy-efficient light bulb by the engineering department.

The credit committee includes the general manager, the controller, sales, the front office, reservations, catering, and the credit manager. Meeting monthly for an hour, the committee reviews those guests and clients of the hotel who were granted credit but have not settled their account. The safety committee typically comprises representatives from human resources, food and beverage, housekeeping, and engineering. Meeting monthly for an hour or so, the committee reviews safety programs and safety records, addresses problems, and discusses the implementation of new safety regulations.

In some full-service hotels, an energy conservation committee includes the chief engineer, resident manager, food and beverage staff, human resource representatives, rooms staff, and housekeeping representatives. The committee typically meets monthly for an hour to discuss strategies and programs for controlling energy costs. Most full-service hotels convene a monthly meeting or at least an annual meeting of all hotel management and employees to review performance and to distribute awards. This event ranges from an hourlong meeting to a company-wide celebration lasting several hours.

As new business practices are evolving as fast as our technologies, resistance to change has become a primary cause of business failure. The future success of a hotel will be driven in large part by the ability to foresee and capitalize on change. As we go through global transitions, the successful hotel will examine the key factors that will not only define success but also the ability to survive in coming years. These key organisational trends must be acknowledged by the successful hotel organisation: visionary leadership, globalization, diversity, flexibility, flat structure, customer focus, zero defects, network orientation, and being in the information fast lane.

The organisation must be able to respond to increasingly globalized sales, the movement to maintaining sales offices in many countries and hotel properties across the globe, and an increasingly globalized labor market. Intercontinental Hotels Group recently introduced a new organisation structure to more efficiently use regional and global resources to drive higher levels of innovation, customer focus, and revenues. Diversity means the organisation must respond to a workforce that is heterogeneous sexually, racially, and chronologically; innovation and conflict/communication issues; and different styles of interaction, dress, presentation, and physical appearance.

Flexibility in the modern hotel organisation means assuring that systems, processes, and people can respond differently to different situations; fewer detailed rules and procedures; greater autonomy and encouragement of initiative; customizing employment relationships to include telecommuting and job-sharing; and lifetime employability rather than lifetime employment. The trend toward flatness in hotel organisations means fewer levels of management, workers empowered to make decisions, and fewer differences in responsibility. The organisation's employees need to believe in a sense of entrepreneurship that reacts proactively to market diversity.

Traditional organisations that follow well-documented rules must give way to leaders who can balance a sense of discipline with one of flexibility. If the customer is king or queen in the 21st century, hotel organisaions will be best served by focusing less on their hotel assets as measures of success and more on their customers. This involves a fundamental shift from viewing the real estate asset as the wealth creator to seeing the customer as the key to building shareholder wealth. A customer focus must reflect business decisions at all levels of developing and operating a hotel organisation. Pursuing such a course will inevitably impact shareholder wealth.

The Japanese concept of zero defects in products and services can yield tremendous benefits for a hotel business organisation. In practical terms, the hotel industry finds it extremely difficult to meet the standard of zero defects in service. Hotel services are based primarily on people, not on computers or other equipment. Twenty years ago, a business executive did not expect a consistent and predictable level of service wherever he or she traveled. Today that is the standard, not the exception, as is the expectation of sophisticated technology in hotel rooms to support business needs. With customer discrimination so acute, it is not surprising that brand loyalty is a diminishing commodity in the hotel industry.

Today's hotel organisation must recognize the need for visionary leadership. The old command-and-control model of leadership is giv-ing way to a focus on leadership in ideas, information, inspiration, vision, and teamwork. A failing hotel organisation is overmanaged and underled. The networked hotel organisation can facilitate direct communication across unit and property boundaries, ignoring the chain of command; cross-unit team structures; outsourcing and downsizing; strategic alliances with competitors and others; customization; and decentralization. Being in the information fast lane is critical.

The traditional role of information technology as a back office support for accounting and bookkeeping has clearly moved to front and center stage. Information technology today influences all aspects of business from corporate strategies to organisational structure. Technology was once viewed as a way to reduce costs by replacing people. That attitude has been firmly supplanted by the idea of seeking information technology support for the creative work all organisations must pursue. Information technology must enable organisations to react more speedily to market needs and, of course, produce the fulfillment of customer demands both quickly and accurately. To do this it must operate on a decentralized basis. Information technology delivers, but it has to deliver the right information to the right people at the right time.

Staffing System

Staffing, which is one of a hotel's most important

management functions, is an ongoing challenge because of the high rate of employee and manager turnover. Full-service hotels can experience annual turnover rates in excess of 100 percent in certain employee classifications. Some managers consider an annual employee turnover rate of 33 percent low. (In other words, in a single year, one-third of a hotel's employees must be replaced.) At this rate, the entire hotel must be completely restaffed every three years. The higher the turnover rate, the larger the number of employees who must be replaced.

In an attempt to reduce employee turnover, hotel and lodging businesses are giving increasing attention to job design, seeking to enhance those job characteristics that give the employee the greatest satisfaction and motivation. Good job design must take into account the needs of employees as well as the demands of the job. Well-thought-out job design begins when management conducts a job analysis-that is, a thorough evaluation of the specific tasks performed for a particular job and the time required to perform them.

Job analysis is an ongoing process, as many jobs change with improvements in technology and pressure to improve product quality. The job analysis is the basis for the job description and job specification. A job description includes the job title, pay, a brief statement of duties and procedures, working conditions, and hours. The job specification is an outline of the qualifications necessary for a particular job. In response to the limits of specialization, organisations can redesign jobs to improve coordination, productivity, and product quality while responding to an employee's needs for learning, challenge, variety, increased responsibility, and achievement.

Such job redesign often involves job rotation, the systematic movement of employees from one job to another; job enlargement, an increase in the number of tasks an employee will do in the job; job enrichment, the attempt to give the employee more control over job-related activities;

and flextime, a flexible work schedule that permits employee input in establishing work schedules. In team-driven job redesign, a concept similar to job rotation, employees can transfer back and forth among teams that provide different services or products. Hotels recruit employees from a variety of sources. Newspapers and employee referrals are used to recruit nonskilled hourly employees.

Supervisory and management employees generally are recruited through colleges and universities, promotions from within, professional associations, and management recruiters. Hotels that take more time in making their selections are more successful in retaining employees. Discussions of employee training and development often concentrate on training techniques without giving a full explanation of what a hotel is trying to accomplish. As training and development impart job skills and educate employees, supervisors, and managers, they also improve current and future employee performance, which affects the bottom line. Effective training includes problem solving, problem analysis, quality measurement and feedback, and team building.

Performance evaluation, also called performance appraisal, is the systematic review of the strengths and weaknesses of an employee's performance. The major difficulty in a performance appraisal is quantifying those strengths and weaknesses. The performance of some jobs is easy to quantify, while for others it is more difficult. An important part of the appraisal process is a well-established job description, so that the employee and the supervisor have similar expectations.

Compensation includes the monetary and nonmonetary rewards that managers, supervisors, and employees receive for performing their jobs. In order to set compensation levels, the human resources department must periodically conduct job evaluations, which determine the value of the job to the hotel. Knowledge of the value of the job to the organisation and of wage rates for each job classification allows the hotel to establish a fair compensation policy.

Job Specialization

Within the lodging industry there are as many degrees of job specialization as there are many types of organisations. One extreme is the case of a hotel where the owner/operator is responsible for checking in the guests, servicing their needs, taking care of the housekeeping for the guest rooms, maintaining the building and grounds, and checking out the guests. There is, to be sure, much to recommend this method of work. It is rewarding to have total control over a project from beginning to end, and many people find it motivating to see the results of their efforts. However, as the demand for additional products or services increases (i.e., if additional rooms are added or another hotel is purchased), it becomes more and more difficult for an individual to do his or her job well.

One benefit of the increased workload is increased revenue, which would enable the individual hotel operator to add housekeeping staff, one or more front desk agents to check in and check out the additional guests, and engineering and maintenance personnel to care for the building and grounds. As a general rule, specialization increases worker productivity and efficiency. On the other hand, delegating jobs increases the need for managerial control and coordination. Someone has to make sure that housekeeping staff come in after the painters have repainted a room, not before! A crucial element of hotel and lodging management is coordinating the many specialized functions within hotels so that the organisation runs smoothly.

Specialization has its own set of problems; it can result in workers performing the same tasks over and over again. A point can be reached where the degree of specialization so narrows a job's scope that the worker finds little joy or satisfaction in it. Signs of overspecialization include workers' loss of interest, lowered morale, increasing error rate, and reduction in service and product quality. One solution to this problem is to modify jobs so that teams can perform them. Instead of a single guest room attendant being assigned to a group of rooms, a work team in a hotel housekeeping department might clean all of the rooms on a particular floor. Some establishments use teams regularly throughout the organisation; others use teams more selectively. Teams can be directed by a manager or can be selfmanaged.

The idea behind self-managed work teams is for workers to become their own managers, which increases their self-reliance as well as develops a talent pool. A concept called the quality circle is based on the belief that the people who actually do the work, rather than their managers, are the ones who are best able to identify, analyze, and correct problems they encounter. The idea originated in Japan in 1962. The quality circle is a group of employees, usually fewer than ten, who perform similar jobs and meet once per week to discuss their work, identify problems, and present possible solutions to those problems.

Career Paths and Opportunities

If you complete your course of study and graduate with a bachelor of science degree in hotel management, most likely you will enter the business at the managerial level. Along the way you will have learned that a successful manager provides clear direction, encourages open communication, coaches and supports people, provides objective recognition, establishes ongoing controls, follows up and gives subordinates feedback, selects the right people to staff the organisation, understands the financial implications of decisions, encourages innovation and new ideas, gives subordinates clear-cut decisions when needed, and consistently demonstrates a high level of integrity.

In a full-service hotel or lodging business, the movement from entry-level position to general manager might encompass 15 years. Career advancement in a limited-service hotel or lodging business can occur more rapidly. A career in a limited-service hotel or lodging establishment might commence at the assistant general manager level, with movement to general manager within three years and to district or regional manager within five to eight years. This accelerated pace is due in large part to the more restricted range of services the manager must master before advancing.

There are three levels of management careers in the hotel or lodging business: first-line, middle, and top.

First-line Management

First-line refers to those who have day-to-day contact with the guests and clients of a lodging business. The first-line manager oversees the work of the supervisors and line employees. In a hotel or lodging business, first-line positions may include assistant manager of housekeeping, assistant front office manager, and assistant restaurant manager. First-line managers are responsible for a hotel's basic work, such as checking guests in and out, making up the guests' rooms, and preparing and serving the meals. First-line managers are in daily or near-daily contact with line employees.

Middle Management

Middle management of most hotel or lodging businesses includes the department manager, general manager, and any position between those levels. Depending on the size of the hotel, the regional manager (who supervises the general managers of the hotels in his or her region) can also fall into this category. Unlike first-line managers, those in middle management plan, organise, lead, and control other managers' activities and are responsible for the performance of their departments.

Top Management

Top management comprises a small group of managers such as the chief executive officer, president, or vice president. Top management is responsible for the performance of the entire hotel business as well as for supervision of the middle managers. The top manager is accountable to the owners of the financial resources used by the organisation, such as the stockholders or executive board. As you have already seen, there are numerous attractive careers in the hotel and lodging business. The following is one of the many paths your career might follow:

a) Assistant manager of the reservations department
b) Reservations department manager
c) Rooms department manager
d) Resident manager
e) General manager
f) Regional manager

Organizing, the process of structuring human and physical resources in order to accomplish organizational objectives, involves dividing tasks into jobs, specifying the appropriate department for each job, determining the optimum number of jobs in each department, and delegating authority within and among departments. One of the most critical challenges facing lodging managers today is the development of a responsive organizational structure that is committed to quality.The framework of jobs and departments that make up any organization must be directed toward achieving the organization's objectives.

Role of Supervisor

In the hospitality industry the term supervisor refers to a manager at a lower organizational level who supervises entry-level or other employees who themselves do not have supervisory responsibilities. The workers are expected to do what the boss tells them to do-that's just part of the job, right? But if employees simply do what they are told, why is labor turnover so high, productivity so low, and absenteeism so prevalent? Why is there conflict between labor and management? The truth of the matter is that the boss is in charge of the workers, but that does not guarantee that the workers will put all of their efforts into the job. This is where leadership comes in.

More than one out of every eight Americans now working have worked in a Mc-Donald's since the first one opened over 40 years ago in California. It seems an incredible statistic, but keep in mind that 8 percent of American employees work in foodservice, and many young people find their first job in foodservice or a hotel. You may already have worked in a hospitality operation yourself. The hospitality industry is composed of 70 percent part-time, short-term people. They are "only working here until"-until they get out of high school, until they get out of college, until they have enough money to buy a car, or until an opening comes up someplace else. It is not uncommon to hear a young hourly employee say, "I'll keep this job until I can get a real job," for what they often mean is that they plan to switch from an hourly to a salaried position.

Hotels and restaurants are dependent on large numbers of people to fill low-wage entry-level jobs that have little interest and no perceived future.Washing pots, busing tables, dishing out the same food every day from the same steam table, lifting heavy bags, mopping dirty floors, cleaning rest rooms, straightening up messy rooms left by unheeding customers every single day can become very tiresome. Workers take these jobs either because no special skill, ability, or experience is required, or because nothing else is available. Some of these people consider the work demeaning. Even though they are doing demanding work that is absolutely essential to the operation, management often looks down on them. They are frequently taken for granted, ignored, or spoken to only when reprimanded. Given the nature of the work and the attitudes of management and sometimes of other workers, it is no wonder that turnover is high.

Another level of hourly worker is the skilled or semiskilled: the front desk clerk, the cashier, the bartender, the cook, the waiter and waitress. These jobs are more appealing, the money is better, and there is sometimes a chance for advancement. Yet here, too, you often find temporary workers-students, moonlighters, people who cannot find anything in their own fields-people working there until. Many employers assume that their employee will not stay long, and most of them do not. According to a National Restaurant Association's Restaurant Industry Operations Report, the turnover rate for hourly workers in full-service operations is 100 percent. That means that your typical full-service restaurant will lose every one of its hourly employees during one year and have to fill every position.

There is really no valid stereotype of today's hospitality worker. The industry employs people of all ages and backgrounds. In fact, an already diverse workplace is becoming more diverse than ever. This is due in part to the fact that new workers entering the workforce are overwhelmingly non-Caucasian ethnic minorities, immigrants, and women. Approximately half of the foodservice workforce, as well as a big presence in hotels, are employees from 18 to 34 years old, a group referred to as Generation X. X'ers will work hard, but they will also make certain demands. They want to do work that they consider worthwhile as well as work they enjoy doing.

The employees want their supervisors to let them be more involved by listening to them and by allowing them to participate in decision making. Not surprisingly, employees do not want supervisors to bark orders in a militant fashion, they want training and expect management to invest time and money in their training and development. At least 50 percent of both foodservice and hotel workers are women. There are more women working now than ever before and they are not necessarily satisfied with traditional women's jobs. There are many female bartenders, cooks, and chefs, as well as many other management positions now filled by women. The fastest-growing ethnic groups in the United States are Hispanics, people of Asian origin, and African-Americans, so it is not surprising to see many of these people in hospitality jobs.

Managerial Functions of a Leader

A leader can be defined as someone who guides or influences the actions of his or her employees to reach certain goals. A leader is a person whom people follow voluntarily.What you, as a supervisor,must do is to direct the work of your people in a way that causes them to do it voluntarily.You don't have to be a born leader, you don't have to be magnetic or charismatic; you have to get people to work for you willingly and to the best of their ability. That is what leadership is all about. Although it is true that many leadership skills are innate and that not all managers make great leaders, it is also true that most managers will benefit from leadership training.

Moreover, natural leaders will flourish in an environment that supports their growth and development. Therefore, activities surrounding leadership development are worth the time and expense. Traditional characteristics of leadership development are:

1. We spend millions of dollars teaching managers technical skill and administrative functions.

2. Managers' "numbers" are the primary benchmark for evaluating their successes and failures.
3. Management training programs are more focused on short-term skills than on long-term development processes.

You need to break out of this limited training "box" if you want to develop leaders who can help your businesses grow. There are seven steps to establishing a foundation for leadership development:

1. Commit to investing the time, resources, and money needed to create a culture that supports leadership development.
2. Identify and communicate the differences between management skills and leadership abilities within the organization.
3. Develop quantifiable measurables that support leadership skills. These include percentage of retention, percentage of promotables, and percentage of crosstrained team members.
4. Make leadership skills a focus of management training. These include communication skills (written, verbal, nonverbal, and listening), team-building skills (teamwork, coaching, and feedback), proactive planning skills (transitioning from managing shifts to managing businesses), and interpersonal skills (motivation, delegation, decision making, and problem solving).
5. Implement ongoing programs that focus on leadership skills, such as managing multiple priorities, creating change, and presentation skills.
6. Know that in the right culture, leaders can be found at entry level.
7. Recognize, reward, and celebrate leaders for their passion, dedication, and results.

In theory, you have authority over your people because you have formal authority, or the right to command, given to you by the organization. You are the boss and you have the power, the ability to command. You control the hiring, firing, raises, rewards, discipline, and punishment. In all reality, your authority is anything but absolute. Real authority is conferred on your subordinates, and you have to earn the right to lead them. It is possible for you to be the formal leader of your work group as well as have someone else who is the informal leader actually calling the shots. The relationship between you and your people is a fluid one, subject to many subtle currents and cross-currents between them and you.

If they do not willingly accept your authority, they have many ways of withholding success. They can stay home from work, come in late, drag out the work into overtime, produce inferior products, drive your customers away with rudeness and poor service, break the rules, refuse to do what you tell them to, create crises, and punish you by walking off the job and leaving you in the lurch. Laying down the law, the typical method of control in hospitality operations, does not necessarily maintain authority; on the contrary, it usually creates a negative, nonproductive environment. What it all adds up to is that your job as a supervisor is to direct and oversee a group of transients who are often untrained, all of who are different from each other, and many of whom would rather be working somewhere else.

As a distinguished leadership expert noted, "managers are people who do things right, and leaders are people who do the right things." Think about that for a moment. In other words, managers are involved in being efficient and in mastering routines, whereas leaders are involved in being effective and turning goals into reality. As a supervisor and leader, your job is to do the right things right, to be both efficient and effective. An effective supervisor in the hospitality industry is one whom, first, knows and understands basic principles of management, and second, applies them to managing all the resource operations.

Leadership Style

The term leadership style refers to your pattern of interacting with your subordinates: how you direct and control the work of others, and how you get them to produce the goods and services for which you are responsible. It includes not only your manner of giving instructions, but the methods and techniques you use to motivate your workers and to assure that your instructions are carried out. There are several different forms of leadership style:

—autocratic,

—bureaucratic,

—democratic, and

—laissez-faire being the most popular styles today.

Before choosing a style of leadership, one must identify the pros and cons of each and then decide if it will be the most effective style in the hospitality industry. Autocratic leadership style can be identified with the early, classical approach to management. A supervisor practicing an autocratic style is likely to make decisions without input from staff, to give orders without explanation or defense, and to expect the orders to be obeyed. When this style of leadership is used, employees be-come dependent on supervisors for instructions. The wants and needs of the employees come second to those of the organization and the supervisor. In bureaucratic leadership style, a supervisor manages "by the book."

The leader relies on the property's rules, regulations, and procedures for decisions that he makes. To the employees, their leader appears to be a "police officer." This style is appropriate when the employees can be permitted no discretion in the decisions to be made. Democratic (also called participative) leadership style is almost the reverse of the autocratic style discussed previously. A democratic supervisor wants to share decision-making responsibility. They want to consult with the group members and to solicit their participation in making decisions and resolving problems that affect the employees. The employer strongly considers the opinions of employees and seeks their thoughts and suggestions. All employees are informed about all matters that concern them. One could compare a democratic supervisor to a coach who is leading his or her team.

Laissez-faire (also called free-rein) leadership style refers to a hands-off approach in which the supervisor actually does as little leading as possible. In effect, the laissezfaire supervisor delegates all authority and power to the employees. The supervisor relies on the employees to establish goals, make decisions, and solve problems. At best, the laissez-faire style has limited application to the hospitality industry.

In the hospitality industry, the traditional method of dealing with hourly workers has generally been some variation of the command-obey method combined with carrot-and-stick techniques of reward and punishment. The motivators relied upon to produce the work are money (the carrot) and fear (the stick)-fear of punishment, fear of losing the money by being fired. All too often, the manner of direction is to lay down the law in definite terms, such as cursing, shouting, and threatening as necessary to arouse the proper degree of fear to motivate the worker.

People who practice this autocratic method of managing employees believe that it's the only method that employees will understand. Perhaps that is the way the supervisor was raised, or perhaps it is the only method the supervisor has ever seen in action. In any case, it expresses their view of the people involved that "workers these days are no good."

Some workers are simply bad workers. However, cursing, shouting, and threatening seldom helps them improve. Many workers do respond to a command-obey style of direction, but those workers often come from authoritarian backgrounds and have never known anything else. This style is traditional and military; the style of dictatorship in countries from which some immigrants come. However, for your average American employee, it does not work. It may be enough to keep people on the job but not working to their full capacity.

When coupled with a negative view of the worker, this style of direction and control is far more likely to increase problems than to lessen them, and to backfire by breeding resentment, low morale, and adversary relationships. In extreme cases, the boss and the company become the bad guys, the enemy, and workers give as little as possible and take as much as they can. In response, close supervision and tight control are required to see that nobody gets away with anything. In this type of atmosphere, customer service suffers and patrons go somewhere else.

Some current theories of leadership can be applied in hotel and foodservice settings. These theories emerged in the 1950s and 1960s, following the discovery that making workers happy does not necessarily make them productive. The theories are based on what behavioral scientists, psychologists, and sociologists tell us about human behavior. They explore what causes people to work productively and how this knowledge can be used in managing employees.

Theory X and Theory Y

In the late 1950s, Douglas McGregor of the MIT School of Industrial Management advanced the thesis that business organizations based their management of workers on assumptions about people that were wrong and were actually counterproductive.

He described these faulty assumptions about the average human being as Theory X:

1. They have an inborn dislike of work and will avoid it as much as possible.
2. They must be "coerced, controlled, directed, threatened with punishment" to get the work done.
3. They prefer to be led, avoid responsibility, lack ambition, and want security above all else.

McGregor argues: "These characteristics are not inborn." He believed people behaved this way on the job because they were treated as though these things were true. In fact, he stated, "this is a narrow and unproductive view of human beings," and he proposed Theory Y:

1. Work is as natural as play or rest; people do not dislike it inherently.
2. Control and the threat of punishment are not the only means of getting people to do their jobs. They will work of their own accord toward objectives to which they feel committed.
3. People become committed to objectives that will fulfill inner personal needs, such as self-respect, independence, achievement, recognition, status, and growth.
4. Under the right conditions, people learn not only to accept responsibility, but also to seek it. Lack of ambition, avoidance of responsibility, and the desire for security are not innate human characteristics.
5. Capacity for applying imagination, ingenuity, and creativity to solving on-thejob problems is "widely, not narrowly, distributed in the population."

6. The modern industrial organization uses only a portion of the intellectual potential of the average human being.

Thus, if work could fulfill both the goals of the enterprise and the needs of the workers, they would be self-motivated to produce, and consequently, coercion and the threat of punishment would be unnecessary. Theory X fits the old-style hospitality manager to a T, and it is safe to say that this pattern of thinking is still common in many other industries as well. However, behavioral science theory and management practice have both moved in the direction of Theory Y. Theory Y is a revised view of human nature with emphasis on using the full range of workers' talents, needs, and aspirations to meet the goals of the enterprise.

A popular way of moving toward a Theory Y style of people management is to involve one's workers in certain aspects of management, such as problem solving and decision making.Usually, such involvement is carried out in a group setting: meetings of the workers for the specific purpose of securing their input. The degree of involvement the boss allows or seeks can vary from merely keeping the workers informed of things that affect their work to delegating decision making entirely to the group.

Enthusiasts of a participatory style of leadership believe that the greater the degree of worker participation, the better the decisions and the more likely they are to be carried out. However, others point out that the degree of participation that is appropriate for a given work group will depend on the type of work, the people involved, the nature of the problem, the skill and sensitivity of the leader, and the pressures of time-the situational leadership approach, to be discussed shortly. The degree to which the boss involves the workers may also vary from time to time, depending on circumstances. You are not going to make a group decision when a drunk is making a scene in the dining room or when a fire alarm is going off on the seventh floor.

Situational Leadership Model

In the situational leadership model developed by Kenneth Blanchard and Paul Hersey, leadership behaviors are sorted into two categories: directive behavior and supportive behavior. Directive behavior means telling an employee exactly what you want done, as well as when, where, and how to do it. The focus is to get a job done, and it is best used when employees are learning a new aspect of their jobs. Supportive behavior is meant to show caring and support to your employees by praising, encouraging, listening to their ideas, involving them in decision making, and helping them reach their own solutions. This method is best used when an employee lacks commitment to do a job.

By combining directive and supportive behaviors, Hersey and Blanchard came up with four possible leadership styles for different conditions. When an employee has much commitment or enthusiasm but little competence to do a job, a directing style is needed; this is high on directive and low on supportive behaviors. Suppose that you have a new employee full of enthusiasm who knows little about how to do the job. A directing style is appropriate: You train the new employee by giving multiple instructions, you make the decisions, you solve the problems, and you closely supervise. Enthusiastic beginners need this direction. A directing style is also appropriate when a decision has to be made quickly and there is some risk involved, such as when there is a fire and you need to get your employees out of danger.

As new employees get into their jobs, they often lose some of their initial excitement when they realize that the job is more difficult or not as interesting as they originally envisioned. This is the time to use a coaching style, with lots of directive behaviors to continue to build skills and supportive behaviors to build commitment. In addition to providing much direct supervision, you provide support.

You listen, you encourage, you praise, you ask for input and ideas, and you consult with the employee. As employees become technically competent on the job, their commitment frequently wavers between enthusiasm and uncertainty.

In a situation like this, the use of a supporting style that is high on supportive behaviors and low on directive behaviors is required. If an employee shows both commitment and competence, a delegating style is suitable. A delegating style of leadership is low on directive and supportive behaviors because you are turning over responsibility for day-to-day decision making to the employee doing the job. These employees don't need much direction, and they provide much of their own support. Using this view of situational leadership, you need to assess the competence and commitment level of your employee in relation to the task at hand before choosing an appropriate leadership style.

As a supervisor, your goal should be to build your employees' competence and commitment levels to the point where you are using less time-consuming styles, such as supporting and delegating, and getting quality results.

Table 1. Situational Leadership

When an Employee Demonstrates:	Use:
Low competence, high commitment	Directing leadership: high directive, low supportive
Some competence, low commitment	Coaching leadership: high directive, high supportive
High competence, variable commitment	Supporting leadership: low directive, high supportive
High competence,	Delegating leadership:

high commitment	low directive, low supportive

Transformational Nature

Leadership is a process that is either transactional or transformational in nature.Transactional leaders motivate workers by appealing to their self-interest. In other words, workers do their jobs and give their compliance in return for rewards such as pay and status. Transactional leaders stress communication of job assignments, work standards, goals, and so on, in order to maintain the status quo. On the other side of the fence are informational leaders. Instead of using rewards and incentives to motivate employees, transformational leaders do the following.

1. Communicate with and inspire workers about the mission and objectives of the company.
2. Provide workers with meaningful, interesting, and challenging jobs.
3. Act as a coach and mentor to support, develop, and empower workers.
4. Lead by example.

By appealing to workers' higher-order needs, transformational leaders gain much loyalty that is especially useful in times of change.

Applying theory to reality is going to be something you work out for yourself. No one can teach you. Since even the theorists disagree among themselves, the choice is wide open. But don't throw it all out; a lot of what the behavioral scientists are saying can be very useful to you. There does seem to be general agreement, supported by research and experience, that the assumptions Theory X makes about people are, at best, unproductive and at worst counterproductive, if not downright destructive. However, an authoritarian style of leadership can be effective and even necessary in many situations, and there is actually no reason why it cannot be combined with a high concern for the workers and achieve good results.

As for Theory Y, probably two-thirds of the workforce has the potential for a Theory Y type of motivation-that is, working to satisfy such inner needs as selfrespect, achievement, independence, responsibility, status, and growth. The problem with applying this theory in the hospitality industry is really not the workers. It is the nature of the work, the number of variables you have to deal with (including high worker turnover), the unpredictability of the situation, the tradition of authoritarian carrot-stick management, and the pressures of time.

The pace and pattern of the typical day do not leave much room for group activity or for planning and implementing changes in work patterns to provide such motivation. Furthermore, your own supervisor or your company's policies may not give you the freedom to make changes. In conclusion, Theory Y does not always work for everyone. However, it is remarkable what is possible when an imaginative and determined manager sets out to utilize this type of motivation and develop this type of commitment.

The best style of leadership, for you, is whatever works best in terms of these three basics:

— your own personality,

— the workers you supervise, and

— the situations you face.

It should be a situational type of leadership, just as your management style must be a flex style that reacts to situations as they arise.

3

Housekeeping Operations

Staffing is an important sequential function of management. Up until now the executive housekeeper has been concerned with planning and organizing the housekeeping department for the impending opening and operations. Now the executive housekeeper must think about hiring employees within sufficient time to ensure that three of the activities of staffing-selection (including interviewing), orientation, and training-may be completed before opening. Staffing will be a major task of the last two weeks before opening.

The housekeeping manager and laundry manager should now be on board and assisting in the development of various job descriptions. The hotel human resources department would also have been preparing for the hiring event.

Job Specifications : Job specifications should be written as job descriptions are prepared. Job specifications are simple statements of what the various incumbents to positions will be expected to do. An example of a job specification for a section housekeeper is as follows:

Once job specifications have been developed for every position, employee requisitions are prepared for first hirings. Note the designation as to whether the requisition is for a new or a replacement position and the number of employees required for a specific requisition number. The human resources department will advertise, take applications, and screen to fill each requisition by number until all positions are filled.

Staffing Housekeeping Positions : There are several activities involved in staffing a housekeeping operation. Executive housekeepers must select and interview employees, participate in an orientation program, train newly hired employees, and develop employees for future growth. Each area of the United States has its own demographic situations that affect the availability of suitable employees for involvement in housekeeping or environmental service operations. For example, in one area, an exceptionally high response rate from people seeking food service work may occur and a low response rate from people seeking housekeeping positions may occur. In another area, the reverse may be true, and people interested in housekeeping work may far outnumber those interested in food service.

Surveys among hotels or hospitals in your area will indicate the best source for various classifications of employees. Advertising campaigns that will reach these employees are the best method of locating suitable people. Major classified ads associated with mass hirings will specify the need for food service personnel, front desk clerks, food servers, housekeeping personnel, and maintenance people. Such ads may yield surprising results. If the volume of response for housekeeping personnel is insufficient to provide a suitable hiring base, the following sources may be investigated:

1. Local employment agencies
2. Flyers posted on community bulletin boards
3. Local church organizations
4. Neighborhood canvass for friends of recently hired employees

5. Direct radio appeals to local homemakers
6. Organizations for underprivileged ethnic minorities, and mentally disabled people (It should be noted that many mentally disabled persons are completely capable of performing simple housekeeping tasks and are dependable and responsible people seeking an opportunity to perform in a productive capacity.)

If these sources do not produce the volume of applicants necessary to develop a staff, it may become necessary to search for employees in distant areas and to provide regular transportation for them to and from work. If aliens are hired, the department manager must take great care to ensure that they are legal residents of this country and that their green cards are valid. More than one hotel department manager has had an entire staff swept away by the Department of Immigration after hiring people who were illegal aliens. Such unfortunate action has required the immediate assistance of all available employees (including management) to fill in.

Whether you are involved in a mass hiring or in the recruiting of a single employee, a systematic and courteous procedure for processing applicants is essential. The magnitude of such an operation required a near assembly-line technique, but a personable and positive experience for the applicants still had to be maintained. The efficient handling of lines of employees, courteous attendance, personal concern for employee desires, and reference to suitable departments for those unfamiliar with what the hotel or hospital has to offer all become earmarks for how the company will treat its employees. The key to proper handling of applicants is the use of a control system whereby employees are conducted through the steps of application, prescreening, and if qualified, reference to a department for interview.

Even though an employee may desire involvement in one classification of work, he or she may be hired for employment in a different department. Also, employees might not be aware of the possibilities available in a particular department at the time of application or may be unable to locate in desired departments at the time of mass hirings. Employees who perform well should therefore be given the opportunity to transfer to other departments when the opportunities arise.

According to laws regulated by federal and state Fair Employment Practices Agencies (FEPA), no person may be denied the opportunity to submit application for employment for a position of his or her choosing. Not only is the law strict on this point, but companies in any way benefiting from interstate commerce (such as hotels and hospitals) may not discriminate in the hiring of people based on race, color, national origin, or religious preference. Although specific hours and days of the week may be specified, it is a generally accepted fact that hotels and hospitals must maintain personnel operations that provide the opportunity for people to submit applications without prejudice.

Prescreening : The prescreening interview is a staff function normally provided to all hotel or hospital departments by the human resources section of the organization. Prescreening is a preliminary interview process in which unqualified applicants-those applicants who do not meet the criteria for a job as specified in the job specification-special qualifications-are selected (or screened) out. For example, an applicant for a secretarial job that requires the incumbent to take shorthand and be able to type 60 words a minute may be screened out if the applicant is not able to pass a relevant typing and shorthand test.The results of prescreening are usually coded for internal use and are indicated on the Applicant Processing Record.

If a candidate is screened out by the personnel section, he or she should be told the reason immediately and thanked for applying for employment. Applicants who are not screened out should either be referred to a specific department for interview or, if all immediate positions are filled, have their applications placed in a department pending file for future reference. All applicants should be told that hiring decisions will be made by individual department managers based on the best qualifications from among those interviewed. A suggested agenda for a prescreening interview is as follows:

1. The initial contact should be cordial and helpful. Many employees are lost at this stage because of inefficient systems established for handling applicants.
2. During the prescreening interview, try to determine what the employee is seeking, whether such a position is available, or, if not, when such a position might become available.
3. Review the work history as stated on the application to determine whether the applicant meets the obvious physical and mental qualifications, as well as important human qualifications such as emotional stability, personality, honesty, integrity, and reliability.
4. Do not waste time if the applicant is obviously not qualified or if no immediate position is available. When potential vacancies or a backlog of applicants exists, inform the candidate. Be efficient in stating this to the applicant. Always make sure that the applicant gives you a phone number in order that he or she may be called at some future date. Because most applicants seeking employment are actively seeking immediate work, applications more than 30 days old are usually worthless.
5. If at all possible, an immediate interview by the department manager should be held after screening. If this is not possible, a definite appointment should be made for the candidate's interview as soon as possible.

Interviewing an Employee

An interview should be conducted by a manager of the department to which the applicant has been referred. In ongoing operations, it is often wise to also allow the supervisor for whom the new employee will work to visit with the candidate in order that the supervisor may gain a feel for how it would be to work together. The supervisor's view should be considered, since a harmonious relationship at the working level is important. Although the acceptance of an employee remains a prerogative of management, it would be unwise to accept an employee into a position when the supervisor has reservations about the applicant.

Certain personal characteristics should be explored when interviewing an employee. Some of these characteristics are native skills, stability, reliability, experience, attitude toward employment, personality, physical traits, stamina, age, sex, education, previous training, initiative, alertness, appearance, and personal cleanliness. Although employers may not discriminate against race, sex, age, religion, and nationality, overall considerations may involve the capability to lift heavy objects, enter men's or women's restrooms, and so on.

In a housekeeping (or environmental services) department, people should be employed who find enjoyment in housework at home. Remember that character and personality cannot be completely judged from a person's appearance. Also, it should be expected that a person's appearance will never be better than when that person is applying for a job. Letters of recommendation and references should be carefully considered. Seldom will a letter of recommendation be adverse, whereas a telephone call might be most revealing.

If it were necessary to select the most important step in the selection process, interviewing would be it. Interviewing is the step that separates those who will be employed from those who will not. Poor interviewing techniques can make the process more difficult and may produce a result that can be both frustrating and damaging for both parties. In addition, inadequate interviewing will result in gaining incorrect information, being confused about what has been said, suppression of information, and, in some circumstances, complete withdrawal from the process by the candidate. The following is a well-accepted list of the steps for a successful interview process.

1. *Be prepared.* Have a checklist of significant questions ready to ask the candidate. Such questions may be prepared from the body of the job description. This preparation will allow the interviewer to assume the initiative in the interview.
2. *Find a proper place to conduct the interview.*The applicant should be made to feel comfortable.The interview should be conducted in a quiet, relaxing atmosphere where there is privacy that will bring about a confidential conversation.
3. *Practice.* People who conduct interviews should practice interviewing skills periodically. Several managers may get together and discuss interviewing techniques that are to be used.
4. *Be tactful and courteous.* Put the applicant at ease, but also control the discussion and lead to important questions.
5. *Be knowledgeable.* Be thoroughly familiar with the position for which the applicant is interviewing in order that all of the applicant's questions may be answered. Also, have a significant background knowledge in order that general information about the company may be given.
6. *Listen.* Encourage the applicant to talk.This may be done by asking questions that are not likely to be answered by a yes or no. If people are comfortable and

are asked questions about themselves, they will usually speak freely and give information that specific questions will not always bring out. Applicants will usually talk if there is a feeling that they are not being misunderstood.

7. *Observe.* Much can be learned about an applicant just by observing reactions to questions, attitudes about work, and, specifically, attitudes about providing service to others. Observation is a vital step in the interviewing process.

Pitfills

Perhaps of equal importance to the interviewing technique are the following pitfalls, which should be avoided while interviewing.

1. Having a feeling that the employee will be just right based on a few outstanding characteristics rather than on the sum of all characteristics noted.
2. Being influenced by neatness, grooming, expensive clothes, and an extroverted personality-none of which has much to do with housekeeping competency.
3. Overgeneralizing, whereby interviewers assume too much from a single remark (for instance, an applicant's assurance that he or she "really wants to work").
4. Hiring the "boomer," that is, the person who always wants to work in a new property; unfortunately, this type of person changes jobs whenever a new property opens.
5. Projecting your own background and social status into the job requirement.Which school the applicant attended or whether the applicant has the "proper look" is beside the point. It is job performance that is going to count.

6. Confusing strengths with weaknesses, and vice versa. What is construed by one person to be overaggressiveness might be interpreted by another as confidence, ambition, and potential for leadership, the last two traits being in chronic short supply in most housekeeping departments.These are the very characteristics that make it possible for management to promote from within and develop new supervisors and managers.
7. Being impressed by a smooth talker-or the reverse: assuming that silence reflects strength and wisdom. The interviewer should concentrate on what the applicant is saying rather than on how it is being said, then decide whether his or her personality will fit into the organization.
8. Being tempted by overqualified applicants. People with experience and education that far exceed the job requirements may be unable for some reason to get jobs commensurate with their backgrounds. Even if such applicants are not concealing skeletons in the closet, they still tend to become frustrated and dissatisfied with jobs far below their level of abilities. The application of the techniques and avoidance of the pitfalls will be valuable tools in the selection of competent personnel for the housekeeping and environmental service departments.

For many years, the approach of many managers was to write a job description and then fill it by attempting to find the perfect person. This approach may overlook many qualified people, such as disadvantaged people or slow learners. Job descriptions may be analyzed in two ways when filling positions:

1) what is actually required to do the work, and
2) what is desirable. Is the ability to read or write really necessary for the job? Is the ability to learn quickly really necessary?

A person who does not read or write or who is a slow learner can be trained and can make an excellent employee. True, it may take additional time, but the reward will be a loyal employee as well as less turnover. It has been proven many times that those who are disadvantaged or slightly retarded, once trained, will perform consistently well for longer periods.There are agencies who seek out companies that will try to hire such people.

Results

If the results of an interview are negative and rejection is indicated, the candidate should be informed as soon as possible. A pleasant statement, such as "Others interviewed appear to be more qualified," is usually sufficient. This information can be handled in a straightforward and courteous manner and in such a way that the candidate will appreciate the time that has been taken during the interview. When the results of the interview are positive, a statement indicating a favorable impression is most encouraging. However, no commitment should be made until a reference check has been conducted.

Reference Checks : In many cases, reference checks are made only to verify that what has been said in the application and interview is in fact true. Many times applicants are reluctant to explain in detail why previous employment situations have come to an end. It is more important to hear the actual truth about a prior termination from the applicant than it is to hear that they simply have been terminated.

Reference checks, in order of desirability, are as follows:

1. Personal (face-to-face) meetings with previous employers are the least available but provide the most accurate information when they can be arranged.

2. Telephone discussions are the next best and most often used approach. For all positions, an in-depth conversation by telephone between the potential new manager and the prior manager is most desirable; otherwise a simple verification of data is sufficient to ensure honesty.
3. The least desirable reference is the written recommendation, because managers are extremely reluctant to state a frank and honest opinion that may later be used against them in court.

Applicants who are rated successful at an interview should be told that a check of their references will be conducted, and, pending favorable responses, they will be contacted by the personnel department within two days. Applicants who are currently employed normally ask that their current employer not be contacted for a reference check. This request should be honored at all times. Applicants who are currently working usually want to give proper notice to their current employers. If the applicant chooses not to give notice, chances are no notice will be given at the time he or she leaves your hotel.

In some cases, the applicant gives notice and, upon doing so, is "cut loose" immediately. If such is the case, the applicant should be told to contact the department manager immediately in order that the employee may be put to work as soon as possible.

Skills vs. Turnover

There is no perfect interviewer, interviewee, or resultant hiring or rejection decision in regard to an applicant. We can only hope to improve our interviewing skills in order that the greatest degree of success in employee retention can be obtained. The executive housekeeper should expect that 25 percent of initial hires into a housekeeping department will not be employed for more than three months. Some new housekeeping departments have as much as a 75 percent turnover rate in the first three months of operation. Certainly this figure can be improved upon with adequate attention to the interviewing and selection processes.

Informational Orientation Programme

A carefully planned, concerned, and informational orientation program is significant to the first impressions that a new employee will have about the hospital or hotel in general and the housekeeping department in particular. Too often, a new employee is told where the work area and restroom are, given a cursory explanation of the job, then put to work. It is not uncommon to find managers putting employees to work who have not even been processed into the organization, an unfortunate situation that is usually discovered on payday when there is no paycheck for the new employee. Such blatant disregard for the concerns of the employee can only lead to a poor perception of the company.

A planned orientation program will eliminate this type of activity and will bring the employee into the company with personal concern and with a greater possibility for a successful relationship. A good orientation program is usually made up of four phases: employee acquisition, receipt of an employee's handbook, tour of the facility, and an orientation meeting.

Employee Acquisition

Once a person is accepted for employment, the applicant is told to report for work at a given time and place, and that place should be the personnel department. Preemployment procedures can take as much as one-half day, and department managers eager to start new employees to work should allow time for a proper employee acquisition into the organization. At this time it should be ensured that the application is complete and any additional information pertaining to employment history that may be necessary to obtain the necessary work permits and credentials is on hand.

Usually the security department records the entry of a new employee into the staff and provides instructions regarding use of employee entrances, removing parcels from the premises, and employee parking areas. Application for work permits, and drug testing, will be scheduled where applicable. All documents required by the hotel's health and welfare insurer should be completed, and instructions should be given about immediately reporting accidents, no matter how slight, to supervisors. The employee must complete this document and give it to the company.

A computer-printed document called a Personnel Action Form (PAF) indicating all data that are required about the new employee. The PAF is serially numbered, is created from data stored on magnetic discs, and is maintained in the employee's personnel file.When a change has to be made, such as job title, marital status, or rate of pay, the PAF is retrieved from the employee's record, changes are made under the item to be changed, and the corrected PAF is used to change the data in the computer storage. Once new information is stored, a new PAF is created and placed in the employee's record to await the next need for processing. A long-time employee might have many PAFs stored in the personnel file.

When either regular or special performance appraisals are given, the last (most current) PAF will be used to record the appraisal. These forms are usually found on the reverse side of the PAF. Since performance appraisals may signify a raise in pay, the appropriate pay increase information would be indicated on the front side of the PAF. All recordings on PAFs, whether on one side or both, require the submission of data, storage of information, and creation of a new PAF to be stored in the employee's record. The

PAF and performance appraisal system should be thoroughly explained to the new employee, along with assignment of a payroll number. The employer should also explain how and when the staff is paid and when the first paycheck may be expected.

Employee's Handbook

The new employee should be provided with a copy of the hotel or hospital employee's handbook and should be told to read it thoroughly. Since the new housekeeping employee is not working just for the housekeeping department but is to become integrated as a member of the entire staff, reading this handbook is extremely important to ensure that proper instructions in the rules and regulations of the hotel are presented. The handbook should be developed in such a way as to inspire the new employee to become a fully participating member of the organization.

Facility Tour

Upon completion of the acquisition phase, a facility tour should be conducted for one or all new employees. For new facilities, access to the property should be gained within about one week before opening, and many new employees can be taken on a tour simultaneously. It is possible for employees to work in the hotel housekeeping department for years and never to have visited the showroom, dining rooms, ballrooms, or even the executive office areas. A tour of the complete facility melds employees into the total organization, and a complete informative tour should never be neglected.

For ongoing operations, after acquisition, the new employee may be turned over to a department supervisor, who becomes the tour director. An appreciation of the total involvement of each employee is strengthened when a facilities tour is complete and thorough. If necessary, the property tour might be postponed until after the orientation meeting; however, the orientation activity of staffing is not complete until a property tour is conducted.

Employee Orientation Meeting

The orientation meeting should not be conducted until the employee has had an opportunity to become at least partially familiar with the surroundings. Employee orientation meetings that are scheduled too soon fail to answer many questions that will develop within the first two weeks of employment. The meeting should be held in a comfortable setting, with refreshments provided. It is usually conducted by the director of human resources and is attended by as many of the facility managers as possible. Most certainly, the general manager or hospital administration members of the executive committee, the security director, and the new employees' department heads should attend. Each of these managers should have an opportunity to welcome the new employees and give them a chance to associate names with faces. All managers and new employees should wear name tags.

A planned orientation meeting should not be concluded without someone stressing the importance of each position. Every position must have a purpose behind it and is therefore important to the overall functioning of the facility. The orientation meeting should be scheduled to allow for many questions. And there should be someone in attendance who can answer all of them. Although the new employee will be gaining confidence and security in the position as training ends and work is actually performed, informal orientation may continue for quite some time. The formal orientation, however, ends with the orientation meeting (although the facility tour may be conducted after the meeting). Finally, it should be remembered that good orientation procedures lead to worker satisfaction and help quiet the anxieties and fears that a new employee may have.

When a good orientation is neglected, the seeds of dissatisfaction are planted.

Quality of Training

The efficiency and economy with which any department will operate will depend on the ability of each member of the organization to do his or her job. Such ability will depend in part on past experiences, but more commonly it can be credited to the type and quality of training offered. Employees, regardless of past experiences, always need some degree of training before starting a new job. Small institutions may try to avoid training by hiring people who are already trained in the general functions with which they will be involved. However,most institutions recognize the need for training that is specifically oriented toward the new experience, and will have a documented training program.

Some employers of housekeeping personnel find it easier to train completely unskilled and untrained personnel. In such cases, bad or undesirable practices do not have to be trained out of an employee. If an understanding of department standards and policies can be demonstrated by a new employee, that portion of training may be shortened or modified. However, skill and ability must be demonstrated before training can be altered. Finally, training is the best method to communicate the company's way of doing things, without which the new employee may do work contrary to company policy.

First Training

First training of a new employee actually starts with a continuation of department orientation.When a new employee is turned over to the housekeeping or environmental services department, orientation usually continues by familiarizing the employee with department rules and regulations. Many housekeeping departments have their own department employee handbooks. Although these handbooks are for completely different types of organizations, the substance of their publications is essentially the same; both are designed to familiarize each new employee with his or her surroundings. Handbooks should be written in such a way as to inspire employees to become team members, committed to company objectives.

Systematic Approach to Training

Training may be defined as those activities that are designed to help an employee begin performing tasks for which he or she is hired or to help the employee improve performance in a job already assigned. The purpose of training is to enable an employee to begin an assigned job or to improve upon techniques already in use. In hotel or hospital housekeeping operations, there are three basic areas in which training activity should take place: skills, attitudes, and knowledge.

— *Skills Training* : A sample list of skills in which a basic housekeeping employee must be trained follows:

1. *Bed making*: Specific techniques; company policy
2. *Vacuuming*: Techniques; use and care of equipment
3. *Dusting*: Techniques; use of products
4. *Window and mirror cleaning*: Techniques and products
5. *Setup awareness*: Room setups; what a properly serviced room should look like
6. *Bathroom cleaning*: Tub and toilet sanitation; appearance; methods of cleaning and results desired
7. *Daily routine*: An orderly procedure for the conduct of the day's work; daily communications
8. *Caring for and using equipment*: Housekeeper cart; loading

9. *Industrial safety*: Product use; guest safety; fire and other emergencies The best reference for the skills that require training is the job description for which the person is being trained.

— *Attitude Guidance* : Employees need guidance in their attitudes about the work that must be done. They need to be guided in their thinking about rooms that may present a unique problem in cleaning. Attitudes among section housekeepers need to be such that, occasionally, when rooms require extra effort to be brought back to standard, it is viewed as being a part of rendering service to the guest who paid to enjoy the room.

A hotel is meant to be enjoyed and, occasionally, the rooms are left quite messed up. However, as long as they're not vandalized, it's part of the territory. The whole idea of being in the hospitality business is to make the guest's stay as pleasant as possible. The rooms are there to be enjoyed. Positive relationships with various agencies and people also need to be developed. The following is a list of areas in which attitude guidance is important:

1. The guest/patient
2. The department manager and immediate supervisor
3. A guestroom that is in a state of great disarray
4. The hotel and company
5. The uniform
6. Appearance
7. Personal hygiene

— *Meeting Standards*: The most important task of the trainer is to prepare new employees to meet standards. With this aim in mind, sequence of performance in cleaning a guestroom is most important in order that efficiency in accomplishing day-to-day tasks may be developed. In addition, the best method of accomplishing a task should be presented to the new trainee. Once the task has been learned, the next thing is to meet standards, which may not necessarily mean doing the job the way the person has been trained.

— *Knowledge Training* : Areas of knowledge in which the employee needs to be trained are as follows:

1. Thorough knowledge of the hotel layout; employee must be able to give directions and to tell the guest about the hotel, restaurants, and other facilities
2. Knowledge of employee rights and benefits
3. Understanding of grievance procedure
4. Knowing top managers by sight and by name

— *Ongoing Training* : There is a need to conduct ongoing training for all employees, regardless of how long they have been members of the department. There are two instances when additional training is needed:

1) the purchase of new equipment, and
2) change in or unusual employee behavior while on the job.

When new equipment is purchased, employees need to know how the new equipment differs from present equipment, what new skills or knowledge are required to operate the equipment, who will need this knowledge, and when. New equipment may also require new attitudes about work habits. Employee behavior while on the job that is seen as an indicator for additional training may be divided into two categories: events that the manager witnesses and events that the manager is told about by the employees. Events that the manager witnesses that indicate a need for training are frequent employee absence, considerable spoilage of products, carelessness, a high rate of accidents, and resisting direction by supervisors.

Events that the manager might be told about that indicate a need for training are that something doesn't work right (product isn't any good), something is dangerous to work with, something is making work harder. Although training is vital for any organization to function at top efficiency, it is expensive.The money and man-hours expended must therefore be worth the investment. There must be a balance between the dollars spent training employees and the benefits of productivity and high-efficiency performance. A simple method of determining the need for training is to measure performance of workers: Find out what is going on at present on the job, and match this performance with what should be happening.The difference, if any, describes how much training is needed.

In conducting performance analysis, the following question should be asked: Could the employee do the job or task if his or her life depended on the result? If the employee could not do the job even if his or her life depended on the outcome, there is a deficiency of knowledge (DK). If the employee could have done the job if his or her life depended on the outcome, but did not, there is a deficiency of execution (DE). Some of the causes of deficiencies of execution include task interference, lack of feedback (employee doesn't know when the job is being performed correctly or incorrectly), and the balance of consequences (some employees like doing certain tasks better than others).

If either deficiency of knowledge or deficiency of execution exists, training must be conducted.The approach or the method of training may differ, however.Deficiencies of knowledge can be corrected by training the employee to do the job, then observing and correcting as necessary until the task is proficiently performed. Deficiency of execution is usually corrected by searching for the underlying cause of lack of performance, not by teaching the actual task.

Methods of Training

There are numerous methods or ways to conduct training. Each method has its own advantages and disadvantages, which must be weighed in the light of benefits to be gained. Some methods are more expensive than others but are also more effective in terms of time required for comprehension and proficiency that must be developed. Following are some useful methods of training housekeeping personnel.

On-the-Job Training (OJT)

Using on-the-job training (OJT), a technique in which "learning by doing" is the advantage, the instructor demonstrates the procedure and then watches the students perform it.With this technique, one instructor can handle several students. In housekeeping operations, the instructor is usually a GRA who is doing the instructing in the rooms that have been assigned for cleaning that day. The OJT method is not operationally productive until the student is proficient enough in the training tasks to absorb part of the operational load.

Simulation Training

With simulation training, a model room (unrented) is set up and used to train several employees.Whereas OJT requires progress toward daily production of ready rooms, simulation requires that the model room not be rented. In addition, the trainer is not productive in cleaning ready rooms. The advantages of simulation training are that it allows the training process to be stopped, discussed, and repeated if necessary. Simulation is an excellent method, provided the trainer's time is paid for out of training funds, and clean room production is not necessary during the workday.

Coach-Pupil Method

The coach-pupil method is similar to OJT except that each instructor has only one student (a one-to-one relationship). This method is desired, provided that there are enough qualified instructors to have several training units in progress at the same time.

Lecture Method

The lecture method reaches the largest number of students per instructor. Practically all training programs use this type of instruction for certain segments. Unfortunately, the lecture method can be the dullest training technique, and therefore requires instructors who are gifted in presentation capabilities. In addition, space for lectures may be difficult to obtain and may require special facilities.

Conference Method

The conference method of instruction is often referred to as workshop training. This technique involves a group of students who formulate ideas, do problem solving, and report on projects. The conference or workshop technique is excellent for supervisory training.

Demonstrations

When new products or equipment are being introduced, demonstrations are excellent. Many demonstrations may be conducted by vendors and purveyors as a part of the sale of equipment and products. Difficulties may arise when language barriers exist. It is also important that no more information be presented than can be absorbed in a reasonable period of time; otherwise misunderstandings may arise.

Usual Training Aids

Many hotels use training aids in a conference room, or post messages on an employee bulletin board. Aside from the usual training aids such as chalkboards, bulletin boards, charts, graphs, and diagrams, photographs can supply clear and accurate references for how rooms should be set up, maids' carts loaded, and routines accomplished. Most housekeeping operations have films on guest contact and courtesy that may also be used in training. Motion pictures speak directly to many people who may not understand proper procedures from reading about them. Many training techniques may be combined to develop a well-rounded training plan.

It is possible to have two students sitting side by side in a classroom, with one being trained and the other being developed. Recall that the definition of training is preparing a person to do a job for which he or she is hired or to improve upon performance of a current job. Development is preparing a person for advancement or to assume greater responsibility. The techniques are the same, but the end result is quite different.Whereas training begins after orientation of an employee who is hired to do a specific job, upon introduction of new equipment, or upon observation and communication with employees indicating a need for training, development begins with the identification of a specific employee who has shown potential for advancement.

Training for promotion or to improve potential is in fact development and must always include a much neglected type of training -supervisory training. Many forms of developmental training may be given on the property; other forms might include sending candidates to schools and seminars. Developmental training is associated primarily with supervisors and managerial development and may encompass many types of experiences. Development of individuals within the organization looks to future potential and promotion of employees. Specifically, those employees who demonstrate leadership potential should be developed through supervisory training for advancement to positions of greater responsibility.

Unfortunately, many outstanding workers have their performance rewarded by promotion but are given no development training. The excellent section housekeeper who is advanced to the position of senior housekeeper without the benefit of supervisory training is quickly seen to be unhappy and frustrated and may possibly become a loss to the department. It is therefore most essential that individual potential be developed in an orderly and systematic manner, or else this potential may never be recognized.

Even though there will be times that the trainee may be given specific responsibilities to oversee operations, clean guestrooms, or service public areas, advantage should not be taken of the trainee or the situation to the detriment of the development function. Development of new growth in the trainee becomes difficult when the training instructor or coordinator is not only developing a new manager but is also being held responsible for the production of some aspect of housekeeping operations.

Suitable Records

Whether you are conducting a training or a development program, suitable records of training progress should be maintained both by the training supervisor and the student. Periodic evaluations of the student's progress should be conducted, and successful completion of the program should be recognized. Public recognition of achievement will inspire the newly trained or developed employee to achieve standards of performance and to strive for advancement. Once an employee is trained or developed and his or her satisfactory performance has been recognized and recorded, the person should perform satisfactorily to standards.

Future performance may be based on beginning performance after training. If an employee's performance begins to fall short of standards and expectations, there has to be a reason other than lack of skills. The reason for unsatisfactory performance must then be sought out and addressed. This type of follow-up is not possible unless suitable records of training and development are maintained and used for comparison.

Performance Appraisal for Employees

Although evaluation and performance appraisal for employees will occur as work progresses, it is not uncommon to find the design of systems for appraisal as part of organization and staffing functions. This is true because first appraisal and evaluation occurs during training, which is an activity of staffing. Once trainees begin to have their performance appraised, the methods used will continue throughout employment. As a part of training, new employees should be told how, when, and by whom their performances will be evaluated, and should be advised that questions regarding their performance will be regularly answered.

Probationary Period : Initial employment should be probationary in nature, allowing the new employee to improve efficiency to where the designated number of rooms cleaned per day can be achieved in a probationary period. Should a large number of employees be unable to achieve the standard within that time, the standard should be investigated. Should only one or two employees be unable to meet the standard of rooms cleaned per day, an evaluation of the employee in training should either reveal the reason why or indicate the employee as unsuitable for further retention. An employee who, after suitable training, cannot meet a reasonable performance standard should not be allowed to continue employment. Similarly, an employee who has met required performance standards in the specified probationary period should be continued into regular employment status and thus achieve a reasonable degree of security in employment.

Evaluation of personnel

Evaluation of personnel is an attempt to measure selected traits, characteristics, and productivity. Unfortunately, evaluations are generally objective in nature, and raters are seldom trained in the art of subjective evaluation. Initiative, self-control, and leadership ability do not lend themselves to measurement; therefore such characteristics are estimated. How well they are estimated depends to a great extent on the person doing the estimating. Two raters using the same form and rating the same person will probably arrive at different conclusions. Certain policies on the use of evaluations should be established so that they are understood by both the person doing the evaluating and the person being evaluated. These policies must be established and disseminated by management.

Reliable evaluations require careful planning and take considerable time, skill, and work. An evaluation must be understood by the employee. Evaluation should be used at the end of a probationary period, and the employee must understand at the beginning of the period that he or she will be observed and evaluated. Each item, as well as what impact the evaluation will have on future employment, should be explained to the employee. People undergoing periodic evaluations, such as at the end of one year's employment, should also know why evaluations are being conducted and what may result from the evaluation.

4

Waste Reduction in Hotels and Motels

The hospitality industry has always been concerned about the environment. In the past, the industry was satisfied to organize and manage an efficient waste removal system, now they are challenged by changing methods and costs of disposing of waste. Laws and regulations are establishing how businesses dispose of their waste. In addition, landfill space is becoming increasingly expensive due to new rules and regulations and in turn, fewer are being built. Businesses must now reevaluate their waste handling practices.

Other external forces are also impacting the way the lodging and hospitality industries handle their waste. There is a steady movement of "green consumerism" from hotel guests, businesses and tourist related industries. Green consumers are asking questions related to the hotel's environmental practices including waste handling, energy and water management, before selecting a site for vacations and conferences.

The travel industry also has joined the movement and is developing a rating system for hotels and resorts based on environmental practices. The hospitality industry is being forced to join the "green movement" or loose their market share of the "green consumer." Stewardship of natural resources and making business decisions based on sound environmental practices have enabled certain proactive hotel companies to tap into the ever increasing "green consumer" market.

Waste reduction includes all actions taken to reduce the amount and/or toxicity of waste. It includes waste prevention, recycling, cornposting and the purchase of products that have recycled content or produce less waste. Waste prevention is one of the easiest methods of reducing waste and can be controlled at the time of purchasing products and services. There is a direct correlation between what a hotel purchases and what it throws away. In addition, all of the resources and economic costs of materials, manufacturing, labor, transportation, packaging, storage and disposal are wasted when a product is discarded.

Cornposting food waste and yard trimmings can save a hotel money on hauling and landfilling fees. However, cornposting is limited by land space at the hotel and/or availability of commercial cornposting sites. Purchasing products made with recycled content creates outlets or markets for the materials collected in the hotel's recycling program. As such, procurement sustains the recycling process and in turn, reduces the amount of waste going to the landfill.

Benefits of Waste Reduction

Following are the benefits of waste reduction:

— savings through reduced purchasing costs,

— reduced waste disposal costs,

— reduced energy consumption and pollution,

— conservation of natural resources.

Recycling is the process by which materials, otherwise destined for disposal, are collected and used as raw materials for new products. Recycling prevents useful materials from being landfilled or combusted, thus saving energy and natural resources.

There are three steps in recycling:

1) collecting the recyclable components of solid waste,
2) processing and manufacturing them into reusable products,
3) purchasing and using the products made with reprocessed materials.

Hotel recycling programs focus on collecting recyclable materials from the hotel's waste stream for recycling and purchasing products made from recycled materials.

Benefits of Recycling:

— reduces hotel waste disposal costs by diverting

— materials from the landfill,

— possibly provides revenues through the sale of

— recyclable materials,

— demonstrates a hotel's commitment to environmental protection to guests, businesses and employees.

Waste Reduction Initiatives

Hotel and motel owners, managers and employees must make a commitment to the hotel's waste reduction and recycling initiatives if these programs are to be successful. To be successful requires initial research in present purchasing and waste handling practices. This includes the cost of disposing of waste, research of products, packaging, vendors, recycling processors equipment and related areas. Further planning is needed in program implementation and employee training. The following actions are suggested to assist in organizing hotels waste reduction initiatives.

— Inform appropriate people in the hotel's corporate structure of the program's progress, emphasizing the savings in waste disposal costs, revenue from material sales, the conservation of natural, non-renewable resources and pollution prevention. Seek their commitment and financial support.

— Appoint a waste reduction manager to provide leadership to each of these initiatives.

— Establish an accounting system that reflects monthly waste management costs.

— Establish a budget for the recycling initiative. Funds may be needed for purchasing recycling containers, equipment and developing employee motivation programs.

— Assist management and employees in establishing the hotel's waste reduction and recycling goals. Post the goals on bulletin boards so all employees are informed.

— Create employee interest. Involve them in the initial stages of the program so they will take responsibility.

— Incorporate recycling procedures in employee position descriptions. Include recycling procedures in new employee orientation, employee training programs and staff meetings.

— Inform the recycling program manager of planned structural renovations and equipment replacements. These activities may require special arrangements with haulers and materials processors.

— Develop an environmentally green marketing plan for the hotel. Work with the hotel's marketing company to highlight the hotel's waste reduction efforts in all promotional materials.

— Inform employees of the program's progress. Place copies of monthly recycling reports on employee bulletin boards and discuss in employee meetings.

Waste Reduction Manager

The recycling program manager is usually appointed by the hotel's general manager. This position requires an individual with leadership and communications skills who is able to motivate employees. Knowledge of the hotel's present purchasing and waste disposal practices and contract procedures would be helpful. The following actions will assist in assuring success.

— Meet monthly with the hotel's general manager to inform him/her of the program's progress.

— Present reports of program progress at department managers meetings.

— Work with management to establish a budget for program organization, equipment purchases and employee motivation/rewards.

— Develop recycling procedures to complement the operational practices of the hotel.

— Work with the recycling materials processor to develop a training program on materials preparation and train employees in recycling procedures specific for the hotel and various departments.

— Research recycling container types and equipment prices.

— With the assistance of department managers and employees, design materials collection and storage systems that complement employee work procedures.

— Issue bid invitations to waste haulers and intermediate processors for recycling materials removal/hauling and processing.

— Issue bid invitations for purchasing and leasing recycling containers and equipment.

— Review existing purchasing practices to determine how purchasing decisions impact the hotel's waste disposal costs.

— Develop a monitoring system that addresses employee compliance in the hotel's waste reduction initiative.
— Review guest comment cards monthly. It is important to know how guests perceive the program.
— Inform employees of the program's progress.
— Seek their ideas and opinions at meetings and in private conversations. Keep them in the loop.
— Evaluate the program's progress often and make adjustments as needed.

Involving all Employees

No matter how well planned your waste reduction and recycling initiatives may be, they probably won't succeed without the support of the hotel department managers and staff. Successful hotel recycling programs require employee involvement, training and recognition. Involve all employees in the recycling program. They are already disposing of waste as they perform their daily jobs.

Recycling is simply disposing of job related waste in a different container from the one used for trash. Seek their ideas in organizing the recycling program and for methods of collecting and storing the materials. Employees are more likely to support a program that they understand and have helped design. Develop motivational programs that create opportunities for staff involvement and enthusiasm about the recycling program.

Training Programmes

Develop employee training programs that include recycling techniques specific for various departments. Include recycling information in new employee orientation programs. Inform employees of environmental issues and laws. Employees want to know why the hotel is recycling.

Recognition. Develop a system of on-the-spot, weekly and monthly incentives for employees who exhibit activity and leadership in recycling and waste reduction efforts. Recognize employees and departments that show exceptional involvement in the recycling program.

Involving Guests

Hotel guests are becoming more environmentally conscious, They are becoming more inclined to support "green" initiatives in the travel and hospitality industry. Most guests are pleased to see the use of products made from recycled materials, energy efficient light bulbs, low-flow shower heads andrecycling programs in hotels and restaurants that they patronize.

Hotel managers report that most guests are willing to participate in the hotel's recycling efforts. To increase guest involvement in the program, place recycling instructions in guest rooms and locate recycling collection containers in convenient locations in convention halls and public areas throughout the hotel. Always place a trash container along side of the recycling container in public areas to avoid trash being thrown in the recycling bin.

Guidelines for Waste Reduction

Waste Reduction guidelines will assist hotel and motel management and employees in reducing the volume and toxicity of waste generated in offices. To successfully reduce waste disposal costs, conduct an audit to determine the types and volumes of waste generated in offices. Plan your waste reduction initiative to target specific products or materials that contribute the greatest volume and/or weight to the waste stream or which create disposal problems. Establish short and long term departmental goals for waste reduction. The following check list provides a format for your department's audit and additional ideas for waste reduction.

Reduce Paper Waste

— Use a centrally-placed or electronic bulletin board for messages instead of making multiple copies of memos.

— Shred office paper and use it to package shipments.

— Eliminate fax cover sheets by using a rubber stamp or sticky notes designed for fax use.

— Reuse envelopes and folders for routing inhouse mail and correspondence.

— Include a statement requesting electronic addresses on all written correspondence.

— Electronic mail will save on postage, labor and paper.

— Decrease the number of hard copies of documents by establishing a central filing system to store documents.

— Use electronic mail for correspondence when possible.

— Prepare documents with small margins and double sided printing or copying.

— Make double sided copies when possible.

— Use the back side of paper that is printed on one side for drafts.

— Make scratch pads from paper used on one side by stacking paper and coating one end with rubber cement and cutting in half.

— Edit and proof read documents on computer screens before printing.

— Use staff routing slips when sharing information in-house to stop multiple copies.

— Purge mailing lists to reduce returned mail.

— This saves on paper use, postage and recycling costs.

— Avoid unnecessary print-outs by faxing directly from the computer.

— Reduce unsolicited mail by sending each solicitor a postcard requesting that they removeyour hotel's address from their mailing list; reuse their original mailing label for your return address.

Reuse:

— polystyrene peanuts, shredded newspapers and

— office paper for packing materials,

— obsolete forms and letterhead for drafts and

— note pads, file folders,

— mugs for coffee instead of disposable cups.

Reduce hazardous waste by purchasing:

— non-toxic inks,

— unbleached and chlorine-free papers,

— nontoxic, biodegradable correction fluid,

— equipment that does not require batteries,

— rechargeable batteries for small calculators

— communication radios and flashlights.

Support recycling by purchasing:

— paper products made from recycled paper (i.e.,

— letterhead, envelopes, computer, copier, fax,and

— laser papers, calculator and cash register

— tapes, file folders, note pads and legal pads),

— recycled office papers and cardstock for pocket

— folders, table tents, business cards, and guest cards,

— file boxes, clipboards, binders, and computer

— diskettes made from recycled materials, furniture, carpet and padding, trash cans, and

- — recycling containers made from recycled plastic,
- — bulletin boards and floor mats made from recycled tires,
- — remanufactured toner cartridges for office, machines (i.e., copiers, laser printers, fax
- — machines, typewriters, cash registers, and ATM machines),
- — refillable pens and pencils rather than throwaways,
- — services from contractors, printers, graphic
- — artists, and other subcontractors who use
- — recycled products and recycle at their businesses.

Waste Reduction Strategies

a) Combine office supply orders; ordering in bulk reduces packaging waste and saves time, energy and money.

b) Chart the shelf life of items (i.e., toner, correction fluid) and purchase only the needed quantity.

c) Request that vendors avoid excessive boxes, bags and wrappings when shipping to your property.

d) Purchase plain paper fax machines. Most documents received on thermal paper are copied and the thermal paper fax is then discarded.

e) Thermal fax paper is not recyclable.

f) Organize a recycling program to recycle all office paper including cardboard, magazinesbrochures, telephone books and computer papers.

g) Recycle typewriter, adding machine and computer ribbons and printer cartridges.

— When you purchase new office equipment, ask about their energy efficiency.

Guidelines for Housekeeping

Waste Reduction Guidelines will assist hotel and motel housekeeping managers in reducing the volume and toxicity of wastes generated in the housekeeping department. To successfully reduce disposal costs, conduct a departmental audit to determine the types and volumes of wastes

— generated for disposal. Plan your waste reduction initiatives by targeting specific products or materials that contribute

— the greatest volume and/or weight to the waste stream or which create disposal problems. Establish short and long

— term department goals for waste reduction and implement appropriate waste reduction strategies.

The following check list will provide a format for your department's audit and provide additional ideas for waste reduction.

— Select vendors who take back reusable containers, pallets and other waste packaging.

— Request that manufacturers package products in returnable and/or reusable boxes and crates.

— Reuse plastic drums and buckets for recycling or trash collection containers in back of the house service areas.

— Use refillable bath soap, shampoo, hair rinse and hand lotion dispensers for guest rooms to eliminate soap pieces and plastic bottles

— Offer newspapers in centrally located places such as lobbies, restaurants, and news stands rather than distributing them to each guest room to reduce the volume of discarded newspapers and plastic bags.

— Eliminate plastic bags and stickers on newspapers.

— Eliminate the use of plastic liners in ice buckets.

— Refinish and reupholster damaged and dated furniture.

Remanufacture worn mattresses

Mattress manufacturers will rebuild to the hotel's specifications. Replace tissues in bathrooms when they are almost empty or leave new rolls or boxes of tissues for the guest to replace. If company policy is to replace half rolls of toilet tissue, save them and donate to shelters or use in employee restrooms. Provide amenities such as shower caps, shoe wipes on request.

— Use the small concentrate empties for spray bottles for cleaning solutions by adding pumps.

— Redye stained bath towels and wash cloths for reuse as pool towels and cleaning cloths.

— Redye linens and carpet to match remodeled decor.

— Rotate draperies to expose different portions to sunlight and extend their useful life.

— Use reusable baskets or plastic containers for guest laundry, thus avoiding disposable paper or plastic wrap

— Use clothes hangers left by guests for employee uniforms or return to the dry cleaners and recycle plastic garment bags.

— Purchase cleaning and laundry products in concentrated form, dilute and pour into reusable containers for individual use.

— Purchase vacuum cleaners with reusable bags vs. disposables ones.

— Purchase sheets with a high thread count for longer wear.

— Provide reusable drinking glasses and coffee cups for guests instead of paper or plastic throwaways.

— Organize a recycling program for metal, plastic, glass and paper materials.

— Use pump-style sprays instead of aerosol cans.

Reduce Toxicity

— Purchase cleaning products with less hazardous constituents.

— Train employees in proper use of cleaning supplies including the dangers of mixing bleach with other cleaning products.

— Label all cleaning supply bottles with appropriate labels.

— Use a hazardous chemical containment pan to prevent leaching of unused chemicals.

— Check chemical containers periodically for leaks and spills and replace as needed.

— Store unused portions in original containers in a cool, dry place away from equipment, and keep storage areas well ventilated.

— Check labels on room deodorizers for hazardous chemical content. Deodorizers are often used to mask smoke and mildew odors.

— Reduce the need for these products by implementing practices, such as changing air conditioning filters every three to four weeks; sealing cracks around windows, doors, and air conditioning units; and operating air conditioning equipment at temperatures recommended by the engineering department.

Support recycling by purchasing:

— Toilet and facial tissues and paper towels made from recycled paper fibers.

— Housekeeping carts, waste containers, caddies, and mop buckets made from recycled plastics.

— Carpet, carpet padding, mats, vertical blinds, and furniture made from recycled materials.

— Dispose of chemicals per label instructions.

— Call your county environmental protection office if you are unsure of how to dispose of hazardous wastes properly.

— Collect dead alkaline, dry cell and rechargeable batteries used in department radios, flashlights and calculators at a central collection point and dispose of them at the battery recycling area in your county.

— Reduce the need for pesticide applications in guest rooms and employee work areas by removing food containers, garbage and recycling containers daily; clean employee break rooms daily to remove crumbs and spills; and report cracks around doors and windows to the engineering department for repairs to prevent crawling pests from entering

Guidelines for Food and Beverage

Waste Reduction Guidelines will assist hotel and motel food and beverage managers in reducing the volume and toxicity of wastes generated by the food service operations. To successfully reduce waste disposal costs, conduct a departmental audit to determine the types and volumes of wastes generated for disposal. Plan your waste reduction initiatives by targeting specific products or materials that contribute the greatest volume and/or weight to your departments waste stream or which create disposal problems. Establish short and long term departmental goals for waste reduction and implement appropriate waste reduction strategies.

— Use reusable metal or nylon coffee filters.

— Use only reusable dishes and flatware in restaurants and employee cafeteria.

— Install a magnet on food waste containers to recover silverware accidently thrown away with food waste.

— Use paper towel dispensers in employee rest rooms that control the amount of paper being dispensed or use less than standard width paper to reduce paper waste as well as litter.

— Use filters in deep fryers to extend the life of cooking oil.

— Distribute condiments, paper napkins, and straws upon request instead of offering them self-serve for take-outs.

— Replace individually wrapped condiment packages with bulk dispensers in restaurants and employee cafeterias.

— Use washable hats and aprons for kitchen employees instead of disposable paper ones.

— Use only cloth napkins, tablecloths and china for restaurants, meetings, and conventions.

— Use stained wash cloths and towels for cleaning rather than paper towels.

— Redye tablecloths and napkins to match new color schemes when remodeling; reuse worn table linens as cleaning rags or remake into aprons, laundry bags, mattress covers.

— Use glass or plastic coasters to reduce cocktail napkin waste.

— Eliminate paper place mats and use cloth ones.

— Reuse five gallon PVC buckets.

— Request fruits, vegetables and meats to be packaged in reusable crates, or recyclable boxes.

Purchase:

— condiments in bulk and dispense the items in smaller, refillable containers.

— concentrate bar mixes; reconstitute and serve from reusable containers.

— dispenser beverages (i.e., juice, iced tea, hot chocolate) in concentrate or bulk and pour into reusable serving containers.

— milk in five (5) gallon dispenser bags delivered in reusable plastic crates, rather than by the gallon. If milk is purchased by the gallon, select recyclable plastic jugs, not waxed cartons.

— frozen foods in bulk and store unserved portions in airtight reusable food containers.

— flours and grains in bulk and store properly in reusable food containers.

— draft beer in returnable/refillable kegs to reduce the quantity of bottles and cans requiring disposal.

— carbonated fountain beverages in refillable cylinders and dispense into reusable glasses.

— beverages with the least distribution packaging.

Reduce Toxicity

— Purchase cleaning products that contain the least amount of hazardous chemicals.

— Use pump-style spray containers for cleaning products.

— Dispose of unused portions of cleaning products according to the labels.

— Dispose of used appliances to scrap dealers who recycle CFC's.

— Purchase refrigerators, freezers, and coolers which are CFC-free.

— Use dry, concentrated dishwasher chemicals in dispensers to reduce chemical spills and waste.

— Reduce the need for pesticide applications by eliminating clutter where pests might hide; sealing cracks around doors where pests may enter; and removing garbage, recycling bins and open food containers at closing time.

— Wipe down all food preparation surfaces, tables and other areas which might contain crumbs to attract pests.

Support recycling by purchasing:

— recycled paper for menus, table tents, guest checks, inventory sheets, calculator and cash register tapes; use the recycling symbol on printed materials to inform guest of your hotel's commitment to the environment.

— paper napkins, place mats, and paper towels are used, purchase ones made from recycled paper.

— serving carts and food storage containers made from recycled plastic and recycle them when they need replacing.

— reusable food storage containers made from recycled materials.

— floor mats made from recycled rubber tires.

— carpet, vertical blinds, and furniture made from recycled materials.

— waste and recycling containers made from recycled plastics.

Guidelines for Energy Efficiency

The hotel industry is equipped with energy intensive equipment and lighting. Air conditioning, heating, lighting, ventilation, refrigeration, motors, cooking, laundry, cleaning and office equipment are necessary for hotel operations. Choices made when purchasing equipment can have a major impact on the hotel's operating expenses and on the environment; therefore, it is important that efficiency be considered before purchasing energy intensive equipment.

Air conditioning (A/C) Efficiency

— Purchase A/C equipment sized for the area of use.

— Look for a high Energy Efficiency Rating (EER); a Seasonal Energy Efficiency Rating (SEER) of 10 or higher is recommended.

— Use high efficiency motors for A/C air handling unit fans (fan speeds).

— Install heat recovery units on large A/C systems to preheat water.

— Compare efficiency of gas and electric air conditioning systems before making a selection.

— Purchase washable, commercial grade A/C filters and change them every four weeks during hot humid months.

Lighting Efficiency

— In purchasing light bulbs, as a general rule, the bulb cost is the smallest cost. Energy costs over a bulb's useful life are many times the original purchase cost. Evaluate bulbs by comparing lumens per watt.

— Convert inefficient incandescent bulbs to efficient fluorescent bulbs in exit signs, guest room lamps and other areas where incandescent bulbs are used.

— The newer 95-watt incandescent bulb replaces the older type 100-watt incandescent bulb.

— Replace incandescent reflector bulbs with lower wattage ellipsoidal reflector bulbs.

— Install lighting controls (timers or occupancy sensors) to turn off lights in unoccupied areas such as storage rooms, employee rest rooms, walk-in coolers, etc.

Increase the energy efficiency of fluorescent lighting systems by purchasing:

- high efficiency fluorescent bulbs; for example, replace a T-8 with a T-12 bulb,
- energy efficient ballasts that provide a more efficient energy transfer,
- reflectors that direct more light out of the fixture into the room,
- high intensity discharge bulbs (Low Pressure and High Pressure Sodium and Metal Halide) for parking lot lighting,
- security lighting, and for select indoor use,
- photovoltaic lighting systems for lighting advertising signs, walkways, plants, trees, decorative water fountains and remote out-door areas.

Electric Motor Efficiency

- Choose high efficiency motors with variable speed controls.
- Consider the hours the system needs to operate before selecting motor sizes.
- Consult with a qualified energy engineer for a costsavings analysis; two small motors may operate more efficiently than one large motor.

Kitchen equipment considerations include purchasing:

- air-miser hoods that use outside air as make-up air
- instead of discharging conditioned inside air,
- a timer for the kitchen exhaust hood that turns off the system when the kitchen is closed,
- smaller convection ovens to replace oversized conventional ovens,
- an air-to-water heat pump water heater for kitchen use,
- refrigeration equipment with high energy efficiency ratings,

Water use considerations:

Water use in hotels varies depending on geographical location, occupancy, property type and season of the year. The average water use is 218 gallons per occupied room per day. Larger properties use more water due to the water intensive facilities often found in the larger hotels, i.e., pools, laundries and restaurants. Excessive use of water increases the cost of operation, increases electrical energy required for pumps, depletes the water supply and puts extra demands on waste water disposal plants.

Increase water use efficiency by purchasing:

— dishwashing machines that use final rinse water for the prewash of the next load of dishes,

— water-saving showerheads and sink faucet aerators: 2.5 gallons per minute (GPM) showerhead and 1.5 GPM aerators are recommended for water savings and guest satisfaction respectively. Showerheads with less water flow often increase the number of guest complaints,

— a food-thawing machine instead of running water over foods for faster thawing,

— laundry washers which use final rinse water for prewashing of the next load of laundry,

— asking guests how often they would like their bed linens and towels laundered.. Some hotels are changing sheets every two to three days and towels every other day.

Materials for Recycling

All hotels and motels have sufficient quantities of recyclable materials to justify recycling. 50-65% of a hotel's waste is recyclable. The amount of recyclables generated in hotels/ motels depends on the following: the type hotel property, occupancy, number and size of meal functions, lounge/bar business, conventions, guest and employee activities and purchasing practices. The type and number of businesses operating in leased spaces in the facility also impact the volume of recyclable materials.

Leased Space

Hotels rent space to a variety of businesses but the most common ones are retail stores, business services and photography operations. Businesses leasing spaces in hotels are often overlooked in recycling programs. Their waste is usually handled by the hotel; therefore, they increase the hotel's waste volume. Consider the amount and type of waste created by a business when negotiating a lease. Cardboard and office paper are the most common and most desirable types of waste created by these businesses.

— If a tenant produces hazardous waste, the hotel may want to require them to handle their own waste disposal.

— Hazardous waste usually requires special disposal containers and transportation. Inquire about how they plan to handle it and request proof of proper disposal. If hazardous waste is thrown into the hotel's waste collection or recycling containers, the hotel may be held responsible for disposal problems.

Waste Audit

A waste audit identifies the types and approximate quantities of materials for recycling and potential savings due to waste disposal cost reduction. An audit helps identify the size containers needed for collecting and storing the recyclable materials at specific sites in the hotel and at the Central Recycling Center. Although an estimate of the amount of recyclables can be done by direct sorting and weighing of waste, previous hotel recycling programs have proven that an acceptable estimate of recyclables can be made from reviewing purchasing and waste removal records and by evaluating the amount and types of waste generated in each department.

The amount of waste and recyclables produced in a hotel is affected by variables that differ every day. A hotel waste audit, depending on type, produces only information related to the waste and recyclables generated on the day of the audit.

Marketing the Materials

Before a hotel recycling program can be implemented, a decision must be made about where the recyclable materials are to be taken for processing. This decision can make the difference between simply disposing of recyclables and receiving money for them. Processors may require different amounts of material preparation required for recycling. This important decision usually involves public or private processing facilities. An intermediate processor collects, consolidates, and prepares quantities of recyclable materials for shipment to manufacturers.

Some processing facilities are owned and operated by mills or manufacturers and others are operated by small companies and individuals. Processors offer different levels of services. Some processors operate buy-back centers where materials are weighed and payment is made for specific materials. Full service processors accept all recyclable materials and may offer other services such as container leasing or loan and materials transportation.

A Materials Recovery Facility (MRF) accepts commingled recyclable materials for processing. Most MRFs accept glass, plastic, paper, aluminum and steel materials. Each operation is different so contact MRF managers for information about acceptable materials and the preparation required. (The hotel should not be required to sort any of the materials, except paper, taken to a MRF). Paper must be kept clean and dry and this is not possible if paper is thrown into collection containers filled with bottles and cans. MRFs may be owned and operated by private industry or by city or county governments.

In some states, MRFs are owned by counties and operated by private industry. MRFs may or may not pay for recyclable materials and occasionally there may be sorting or processing fees. Government owned MRFs do not usually pay for recyclable materials. The majority of the privately owned MRFs do not charge for sorting and pay for some of the materials. Each operation is different so a thorough research is advisable before selecting a MRF. Before choosing a processor for your hotel's recyclable materials, investigate the laws, rules and regulations governing hauling and tipping fees in your area. In some areas recycling may be included in waste hauling franchise agreements with cities and counties. Recycling is exempt from waste franchise contracts in most areas.

Central Recycling Center

The Central Recycling Center (CRC) is an area outside the hotel where recyclable materials are stored until they are transported to a processor. In larger hotels CRCs may be located in the dock or receiving area. Consideration should be given to the location of the CRC. For convenience, locate it outside the hotel near an employee service exit. Easy access to the container(s) is needed for vehicles picking up and transporting the materials. The CRC is usually located outside the hotel because of the amount of space required for containers. Odors, insects and rodents are also reasons for locating CRCs outside.

The hotel's design, space limitations and vehicle access may make it impossible to locate CRCs conveniently. Local zoning ordinances may regulate the CRCs location. Visibility of the CRC is a concern for some hotel management. They are concerned with the visibility of recycling equipment and stored materials creating an undesirable appearance for the guests. However, guests are expressing interest in preserving the environment and recycling is one way for the hotel to create a positive environmental image.

CRCs that are visible to guests create a positive image for the hotel. In areas with zoning restrictions CRCs can be concealed with fences, walls or landscaping. Equipment is needed in the CRC to prepare materials and store them until they are hauled to the recycling materials processor. Equipment usually found in the CRC are storage containers such as a large recycling roll-off, dumpster and/or portable 92-gallon containers. The type materials storage container(s) needed depends on the available space, volume of materials to be recycled and the requirements of the processor.

Hotels with food and beverage operations need a baler for reducing the volume of cardboard created from food and drink packaging. A large trash container for disposing of non-recyclables should be placed in the CRC. If a trash container is not available, nonrecyclable materials may be thrown into recycling containers or on the ground.

A roll-off container may be compartmentalized for sorted recyclables or simply one large compartment for commingled materials. They are designed with a closed top and conveniently located doors. The top keeps the materials from blowing out of the container when it is moved and provides security for the materials. A locking system is usually optional, but highly recommended to keep out unwanted garbage and recycling material thefts. Roll-off containers are available in different sizes. To reduce the number of times the container is hauled and/or emptied at the processor, select a roll-off recycling container as large as space permits. If the hotel is paying for each container pull, the savings from recycling is reduced when containers are pulled too often or half full. Recycling roll-off containers are available through manufacturers, waste hauling companies and some material processors and may be purchased or leased.

Dumpsters Waste Containers

Dumpster waste containers are commonly used at smaller hotel/motel properties for storing waste. They are also being used for storing specific recyclable materials such as newspaper, cardboard and office paper. They work satisfactorily for storage of office paper and newspaper. However, dumpsters do not have adequate space to store cardboard or all of the recyclable materials from large hotels. Dumpsters require more frequent emptying, thus increasing the cost of recycling if the hotel is charged for the number of times per week/month the dumpster is emptied.

A recycling dumpster is emptied into a larger container on the back of a truck. The dumpster is not removed from the hotel. Drivers may pick up materials from several locations and dump them into the same container before hauling to the processor or mill. This creates a question as to how the weights are determined. Weights of recyclable materials in dumpsters are usually estimated. Materials are not weighed before dumping into the large container on the truck. If the hotel expects payment for recyclable materials, ask how the weights are determined.

If dumpster type containers are used for collection of recyclables and waste materials at the same location, paint the recycling dumpster a different color and label it. This will help prevent trash/waste materials from being thrown into the recycling container. Dumpster recycling containers may be provided at no cost by some companies or they may be leased or purchased from a waste hauler or intermediate processor.

Portable Storage Containers

Large 92-gallon portable rolling containers are the third type of container used in hotel Central Recycling Centers (CRCs) for collecting and storing materials. These containers are convenient for small hotels/motels that recycle only a few items such as aluminum cans and office paper. They are also used at larger properties for collecting and storing newspaper and office papers. Individual containers have limitations on transportation and storage capacity. This smaller container is usually transported by a recycling company or by a hotel vehicle.

Materials Flow Plan-Routes

Once sites for recycling containers have been identified and storage containers selected, establish a materials flow plan-routes to move the recyclables from the temporary storage sites to the Central Recycling Center. Developing a materials flow plan is a very important step in setting up the recycling program. The flow plan establishes the type materials to be recycled at each location, where materials are to be stored, where collection containers are to be used, which employees perform the work tasks and the direction the materials are to be moved through the property. Complete materials flow plan worksheets for every department and mark the directions the materials are to be moved on a property floor plan.

1. The first step in developing the recycling materials flow plan is to review the hotel's floor plan. Locate the storage spaces, hallways, equipment placement and employee traffic patterns in all departments.
2. Identify collection points at work stations and storage areas. From this information a decision can be made on the placement of storage containers and the size containers for each location.
3. Establish people traffic patterns and routes for moving the recyclables through the hotel. The traffic movement routes should be the ones with the least amount of

interference with hotel guests and employee activities. Materials flow plans should start at the point where the recyclables are generated and continue until the materials are placed in the recycling storage container(s) in the CRC.

Recycling Collection Containers

Involve employees in deciding where the recycling collection containers will be located in their work areas, For greater employee participation in the recycling program, locate collection containers in or near work areas where recyclables are generated. This method is called collecting at the source or point of waste generation. For example, place a recycling collection container near the can opener in the kitchen. When cans are opened and emptied they are easily placed in the appropriate recycling materials collection container.

Hotel design, equipment placement and traffic patterns may prevent the containers from being placed in convenient locations in some departments. In this case, place the containers as close to the work area as possible. To reduce the labor costs of recycling, handle the materials as few times as possible. However, in offices and on guest room floors it is necessary to add an intermediate storage center where materials are temporarily stored during the day until they can be moved to the Central Recycling Center (CRC).

Selecting Recycling Containers

— After the material collection points have been identified, it is time to choose containers.
— Match the containers to materials to be collected and to the identified collection and storage spaces throughout the property.
— Carefully measure the spaces and compare the specifications provided by vendors.

— Consider color coding the containers for specific recyclable materials in a sorted materials recycling program.

Materials Processing Equipment

Materials processing, except for cardboard, is not recommended in hotel recycling programs. Most hotel recycling programs to collect and store recyclable materials until the materials are transported to a processor. If storage space is limited and/or transportation costs are high, materials may need to be processed at the hotels.

A baler is the most frequently used processing equipment in hotel/motel recycling programs and is used to bale cardboard. Cardboard is the most abundant recyclable material in hotels/motels and restaurants. If a baler is not used, the massive amount of cardboard quickly fills recycling roll-offs and dumpsters. This increases the number of times the roll-off or dumpster needs emptying, thus increasing the cost of recycling.

Balers are available from manufacturers, processors and some hauling companies. Purchasing a baler may be as simple as signing a lease/purchase agreement with a processor with the sale of your cardboard paying for the baler. If this is the case, include a clause about market price fluctuations. Economically, purchasing a baler for baling cardboard is a wise decision for most hotels and restaurants. Recycling baled cardboard provides a quick return on the investment in a baler.

Marketing Cardboard

Cardboard is one of the most marketable recyclable materials collected in recycling programs. A recycling program manager will want to check the options in their area before selecting a processor. Many companies will pick up clean, baled cardboard at the hotel and transport it to a processor at no cost to the hotel and pay for the cardboard. Since there are many companies wanting the cardboard, the issues are: price, service and documentation. For documentation of recycling and payments, request weight receipts from the processor.

Collection and Preparation

For a successful hotel recycling program, recycling materials collection and preparation must become the responsibility of every employee. The method of materials collection and preparation in the hotel/motel depends on the degree of preparation required by the processor. A small amount of preparation is required by all processors. Preparation of recyclables at the source is easier and less time consuming. As products are used or containers are emptied, place in specific recycling collection containers instead of a trash container. Even if the materials go to a materials recovery facility (MRF), some sorting and preparation is required.

When evaluating how to collect and where to store recyclables, inquire about local fire codes for storing paper and other materials at intermediate and central recycling centers. There are two ways of collecting and storing recyclables in hotels/motels-sorted and commingled. The method is used in your recycling program depends on the requirements of the processor who is handling your hotel's recyclable materials and the amount of labor the hotel is willing to pay for sorting the materials.

Sorted Materials

In a sorted materials recycling program, materials are sorted by type. Steel, aluminum, plastic, paper and glass are each stored in separate recycling containers. These materials may be sorted further. For example, glass is sorted by color into clear, green and brown.

Commingled Materials

In a commingled recycling program, all the recyclable materials except paper are stored together. Office paper and cardboard are usually an exception because they must be kept clean and dry, so they are stored separately. The commingled materials are sorted and processed at a MRFs. Before employees begin collecting materials and placing them in recycling containers, provide training on procedures for preparing materials. Check with your processor as to the degree of preparation and sorting of materials required.

Basic Materials for Recycling Information

The following recycling guidelines provide basic recycling information for materials preparation. Materials preparation may be slightly different with each processor for specific materials.

Paper

Cardboard is the most important material to recycle in a hotel/motel recycling program. All departments in the hotel produce a large volume of cardboard. Proportionately, cardboard is the largest part of a hotel's waste stream. Because of its bulk, cardboard occupies a tremendous amount of space in waste containers and should be removed from the hotel's waste stream, baled and recycled.

Glass

Glass is primarily generated in the Food and Beverage Department. A small amount of glass may be generated from service bars in guest rooms. Most of the glass comes from beer, wine, liquor and food containers. Some processors require that glass be sorted by color-clear, brown and green. Processors with MRF's accept glass that is commingled. The glass is then color sorted by the processor.

Metal

Metal, aluminum and steel/bimetal, materials for recycling are generated through out the hotel/motel. Soft drink and juice machines contain aluminum cans. Steel/bimetal cans are generated in kitchens and food preparation areas. Equipment made from metal is located in various areas of the property.

Plastic

Plastic is found in the Food and Beverage and Housekeeping Departments. Guests also leave plastic bottles in guest rooms. The Society for Plastics Industry (SPI) developed a standard identification system that identifies different kinds of plastic resins. This helps plastic processors recover different kinds of plastic materials. The coding system has a recycling triangle with number 1-7 which identifies the resin. Originally only plastic bottles were coded, however, now most plastic containers have the recycling symbol on the bottom. Check with your processor as to the type plastics they will accept.

Cooking Oil and Grease

Collect and strain cooking oil and grease from fryers and cooking in kitchens. Companies that recycle cooking oil and grease may provide collection containers for its storage and haul it from the hotel. This service is provided at no cost by some grease recyclers.

Furniture

Recycle used furniture by refinishing and reupholstering it. Furniture can be sold to other hotels, employees or donated to charitable causes. Refinish pool and patio furniture instead of purchasing new furniture. Aluminum patio furniture is recyclable with aluminum cans at most processors.

Equipment

Repair quality used equipment. Recycle old equipment with a metal recycling processor, trade it when purchasing new equipment. Give old equipment to vocational schools for teaching repair techniques to students. Keep it out of the hotel's waste stream.

Motor Oil

Establish a motor oil recycling center in the maintenance department for used oil from equipment motors. Oil collection centers for public use are located throughout the state. Ask your oil supplier about setting up an oil recycling program at the hotel for use by employees and vendors.

Construction Debris

Include collection and disposal of construction materials in contracts. Dispose of construction materials separately from the hotel's regular waste. Construction debris such as windows, doors and lumber are recyclable. Inform contractors of your recycling program and request that they comply while working on the property.

Landscape Waste

Include landscape waste removal in lawn maintenance contracts. If lawns and shrubs are maintained by the hotel establish a landscape recycling program. Shred fronds and clippings to make plant bedding material to save water, moderate soil temperatures, discourage weeds and reduce competition from grass.

5

Hospitality Technology

In the World economy, tourism has emerged as one of world's largest industries and a fastest growing sector. Tourism receipts account for a little over 8% of world export of goods and more than 34% of world export of services. In India, however, the sector has failed to receive due importance on the country's development agenda. Employing only 2.4% of the Indian workforce, the vast potential of tourism as an instrument of employment generation and poverty alleviation has tended to remain largely unutilized.

Of the 625 million world tourist arrivals in 1998, India received a meagre 2.36 million or 0.38% of the total world tourist arrivals and only 0.62% of world tourist receipts. Compared to other countries in the region India's performance in the sector has been rather poor. Major causes cited for the low performance are lack of professionalism, unhygienic conditions, poor infrastructure, lack of easily accessible information, lack of safety, poor visitor experience, restrictive air transport policy, inadequate facilitation services, multiplicity of taxes and the low priority accorded to tourism. However, despite its tiny share of world tourist arrivals, tourism in India has emerged the second largest foreign exchange earner for the country even though the mainstay of the Tourism industry in India continues to be domestic tourism.

Domestic tourists (excluding religious tourists), who stayed in accommodation establishments, increased from 109.2 million in number in 1993 to 159.9 million in 1997, registering an annual rate of growth of 10%. That growth rate declined to 9.35% in 1999 when an estimated 175.4 million domestic tourist visits were recorded. The foreign tourist arrivals to India grew from 1.82 million in 1992-93 to 2.33 million in 1996-97, registering an average annual growth rate of 6.37% during the Eighth Five Year Plan Period.

In first two years of the Ninth Plan, the growth rate declined to 1.49% and an estimated 2.40 million foreign tourist arrivals were recorded in 1998-99. A very large proportion of the foreign tourists, i.e. around 91.7%, visited India for holidaying and sightseeing, followed by business travellers who constituted approximately 5.1% of the visitors. Although international arrivals are a small proportion of world tourist arrivals, international tourists have the longest stay of 29 days in India. This is reflected in the proportion of revenues being higher than percentage of world tourist arrivals. The foreign exchange earnings during the Eighth Plan period surged from Rs. 6,060 crore in 1992-93 to Rs 10,231 crore in 1996-97, achieving an annual growth rate of 13.99%. The growth rate declined to 10.99% in the first two years of the Ninth Plan and earnings in 1998-99 were estimated at Rs. 12,604 crore. The sector provided direct employment to about 14.79 million people during 1998-99.

The Ninth Plan envisages the Government playing a role of facilitator for private sector participation in the development of tourism. The Plan seeks to diversify the tourism product by encouraging rural and village tourism, pilgrim and spiritual tourism, adventure and eco tourism, indigenous and natural health tourism, heritage tourism and youth and senior citizens' packages. The outlay for the Central Sector in the Ninth Plan is Rs. 793.75 crore, comprising a budgetary support of Rs. 485.75 crores and internal and extra budgetary resources of Rs. 308 crores. The main schemes of the Ministry of Tourism relate to infrastructure development, human resource development and publicity and marketing.

Infrastructure Development

Ministry of Tourism has identified 21 circuits and 12 destinations for development. Financial assistance is provided to State/Union Territory (UT) Governments for developing tourist infrastructure at these places. In first three years of the Ninth Plan, 779 projects have been taken up. It has been observed that many States, particularly in the North-Eastern region, could not avail themselves of the financial assistance provided under the scheme because they could not find the required matching contribution for projects prioritized under the scheme.

There is a need for modifying the pattern of funding under the scheme to enable all such States to benefit from it. The scheme stipulates transfer of land ownership in respect of those projects in the name of the Central Government. The stipulation is acting as a deterrent in the operation of the scheme as the States face legal difficulties in transferring the land ownership. Ministry of Tourism needs to take urgent action to waive the condition. The Ministry has envisaged an equity scheme for attracting funds from financial institutions but the scheme has not made much headway because the State Governments have not been able to put up financially viable projects. There is a need to evaluate the scheme.

The hospitality and service sector has assumed high priority with the growth of tourism and the diversification of tourism activities. At present, the Ministry of Tourism is running 21 Institutes of Hotel Management (IHMs) and Catering Technology and 14 Food craft Institutes (FCIs). The

IHMs provide 3-year Diploma in Hotel Management, 1-year Post-Graduate Diploma in Accommodation Operations, 1-1/2 year Post-Graduate Diploma in Dietetics and Hospital Food Science, 1-1/2 year Certificate course in Food Production, 6- month Certificate course in Food & Beverage Services, 6- month Certificate course in Hotel and Catering Management, 1-1/2-year Post Diploma in Hotel Administration and P.G. Diploma in Fast Food Operations.

The FCIs are engaged in providing the craft Diploma in Cookery, Food & Beverage Service/ Restaurant & Counter service, Reception & Book Keeping, House Keeping and Bakery & Confectionery. The trained manpower released during the Eighth Plan period was 7168 persons. The tentative target in the Ninth Plan is to produce 12000 Diploma holders in Hotel Management and 16000 manpower in other crafts courses. A majority of Institutes operated by the Ministry have attained self-sufficiency in meeting the revenue expenditure. No new IHMs are proposed to be set up in the Ninth Plan period. In view of the employment generation potential of the craft level trained manpower, 15 new FCIs are to be set up in the Ninth Plan. The training courses run by the Institutes should be designed to suit the needs of the various target groups.

Tourism Generating Markets

There is fierce competition in tourist generating markets from several nations for attracting traffic to their countries. Ministry of Tourism conducts overseas publicity through a network of 18 Government of India Tourist Offices located abroad. The promotional expenditure on the overseas offices, which was Rs. 47 crore in the terminal year of the Eighth Plan increased in the Ninth Plan period to Rs. 52.2 crores in 1999-2000, accounting for 47.45% of the total plan allocation in that year. There is a need to examine cost effectiveness of the expenditure incurred on overseas publicity. The Ministry of Tourism also provides financial assistance to the State Governments for promotion of select fairs and festivals and rural craft Melas in the country. These fairs and festivals play a positive role in developing tourism by providing cultural glimpses of the States to tourists and generate local income and employment.

Restrictive Air Transport Policy

Air seat capacity constraints have been noticed on several international sectors connecting India. Air India, however, has not been able to take full advantage of the capacity available to it under the various bilateral agreements due to fleet limitations and low level of efficiency. A number of foreign airlines have shown interest in expanding seat capacities on the various sectors. Ministry of Civil Aviation, however, is denying international carriers additional flights for fear of diverting traffic away from Air India. The non-availability of adequate air seat capacity is constraining the growth of tourism in the country. In the interest of the development of tourism and trade, a liberal policy of allowing capacity expansions by scheduled airlines needs to be followed.

Poor Facilitation Services

The facilitation services in the country are quite inadequate. The poor airport facilities are a constraint in the development of tourism. The airport infrastructure services need to be improved and modernized. The Ministry of External Affairs and the Ministry of Home Affairs can consider liberalisation of the system for issue of visa/ permit. Streamlining the process of migration/customs clearance and prevention of touting and misguiding of tourists are also essential.

Multiplicity of Taxes

A multiplicity of taxes exists in the tourism sector. The

quantum of taxes also varies from place to place. This creates hurdle in packaging of the tourism product and is also irksome to the tourist; it makes the product expensive as well. The taxes in the sector, therefore, need to be rationalized and reduced for end-customer to make the destination competitive. Further, some uniformity in taxes on tourist transport should be adopted to facilitate free flow of tourist traffic across the State borders.

Publicity through Internet

In order to make effective use of the resources for overseas publicity, the application of information technology needs to be promoted in the sector. It may be advantageous to close the Government of India Tourist Offices overseas and promote publicity through the Internet and television. The Ministry of Tourism launched a website in January 1999. The tourist offices abroad are likely to become redundant with the improvement of the website. In spite of the repeated role of tourism in employment generation and socioeconomic development in the country, tourism has not attracted the desired priority. It is necessary to focus attention on the potential role of tourism as an effective instrument of employment generation, particularly in backward areas.

Plans and Perspectives

Haphazard and uncontrolled growth can destroy the very base on which tourism is built and poor planning can cause considerable damage as noticed at the places of tourist interest in States of Himachal Pradesh, Goa and Jammu & Kashmir. Tourism development should be based on perspective plans prepared with appropriate technical and professional assistance. The plans/projects must include environmental impact studies, carrying capacity studies, instruments of spatial and land use planning, instruments of architectural controls, strategy for preparing the local community to safeguard its cultural identity and awareness programmes for local participation and local commitment to the project.

Rural tourism needs to be given an impetus by earmarking funds for pilot projects on the basis of a model plan for each State for the purpose. These villages can be taken up for priority development particularly if the projects can be linked with the restoration of heritage properties in the area. This would provide a boost to local performing arts and help conserve the local culture apart from preventing rural-urban migration. 14. Local people in the rural areas should be encouraged to participate in tourism related projects, which may preferably be formulated by the tourist officials in consultation with locals and NGOs. These projects could be in the nature of providing glimpse of the village ambience and the tourists presented with local cuisine, art and culture by persons in local costumes engaging in the daily activities of cooking, weaving, dancing etc.. Moderate, but clean, accommodations for tourists should be constructed by villagers in traditional design and architecture. Bank finances should be made available at attractive terms and conditions for promotion of such projects.

Although the North-East could be developed as a tourist haven by virtue of its topographic advantages, diverse cultures and its pristine areas unspoilt by pollution, tourism development has tended to elude it. The Plan expenditure incurred on the schemes operated in the N.E. States has been only about 30% of the amount sanctioned during first three years of the Ninth Plan. The concept of non-lapsable funds, introduced to ensure utilization of the funds, is meaningless if it does not translate into concrete development. A revision in policy is required.

The financial performance of India Tourism Development Corporation Ltd. (ITDC) improved during the

Eighth Plan period and the net profit after tax increased from Rs. 10.05 crore in 1992-93 to Rs. 55.80 crore in 1996-97. In first two years of the Ninth Plan the profit after tax declined from Rs.43.30 crore in 1997-98 to Rs. 10.81 crore in 1998-99. ITDC would be required to intensify its efforts for economy in expenditure and grabbing more business through new initiatives in the face of competition by private sector.

Impact of New Technologies

Tourists spend considerable time planning their activities, both before they visit and on the visit itself. However, tourists deliberately make plans that are not highly structured and specific, so that they can take advantage of changing circumstances. The new technologies should help tourists to move between the guidebook and planning their activity, such as maps that show some of the 'social structure' of cities, and guides that better support the flexible nature of tourists' plans.

Nearly all individuals in the western world take some sort of holiday away from home every year, although the number of days differs across and within different countries. Tourism is also an activity that can divide rich and poor, through a negative or parasitical effect that damages places: 'touristification'. As one would expect, there is a large body of literature that explores these issues from economic, cultural, environmental and other perspectives.

Some tourism studies have noted that insufficient attention has been paid to the experience and practices of the tourist. Instead, most work has focused on the effects of tourism. Fodness and Murray comment that "detailed knowledge of the basis of actual tourist behaviour [is] lacking", and Aramberri argues that much tourism research "does not help to explain the nature of modern mass tourism". The work that has looked in most detail at tourist practice has been the "tourist information seeking" literature. This literature has tended to avoid detailed qualitative description, focusing more on broad categorisations of tourist practice and questionnaire-based studies. This lack of detailed observations presents a number of problems for the design of technologies.

Specifically, there is a lack of understanding of the methods tourists use to choose and arrange their various activities. This motivated the choice of ethnographic methods to look in depth at how tourists arrange their activities, rather than concentrating on the effects of tourism, as is more traditional. In doing this, the approach is similar to recent studies of museum visitors, interactions between local people and tourists, and tourist information centres. In these cases a focus on the 'how' of ordinary activities, such as looking at a shared museum exhibit, can lead to findings useful for the design of technologies. As the growth in online gaming shows, many leisure technologies take on a new life when designed for group or social interaction.

The cities—Edinburgh and Glasgow, are the second and third most popular cities for tourists to visit in the U.K., after London. Summer is a particularly busy time of the year for both cities, with the Edinburgh Festival (as well as the better weather) a major tourist attraction. While the package tour market is obviously a very important part of tourism, more tourists who arrange their activities themselves, since this group suffers more acutely from problems of organisation. While a major proportion of independent travellers are 'backpackers', young people travelling for a prolonged period of time before entering paid employment, independent travellers are a diverse group with a wide age range.

Problems of Tourists

The first, seemingly straightforward, problem which tourists face in an unfamiliar place is what to do. Unlike work, where tasks are often determined (in part) by an overall goal or by other people's plans, tourism is much more open-ended. Tourism encompasses a broad range of activities such as sightseeing, relaxing, shopping, visiting friends and visiting family. Indeed, since tourism can be part of business travel, the boundary between work and leisure is often blurred. Yet whatever tourists do, they must at least make some sort of decision about what to do, often in advance. This decision must take into account the time it takes to get to different places, as well as balancing the attraction of different sites. Even when one arrives at a tourist 'attraction' this problem reappears at a different scale, e,g. which parts of a large museum to visit?

Along with the question of what to do, tourists need to work out how they are going to do these different activities. When one reaches a tourist site one has to be careful about how one acts, since behavioural norms can be different in different countries. Ignorance about local customs is an oft mocked feature of tourists. Even straightforward activities such as buying goods can be organised differently in different countries, compounded with the problems of working with a new currency, and avoiding being exploited, or just 'looking stupid'.

Along with what and how, tourists have to manage when they do different activities. Tourism is usually constrained in time, because of the need to return home. Time is also a problem in that tourists work with organisations that provide services: opening times must be co-ordinated with the times of public transport, such as trains or buses. This is compounded by the 'pre-booking problem'. Many facilities require pre-booking, so decisions need to be made before one has been to a place.

These two problems in turn interact with the third tourist problem: finding where things are. In visiting a city many of the attractions are distributed around the city. There is therefore a need to avoid spending too much time travelling between places, understand what one might see and do along the way, and group together attractions which are close together. In doing so tourists must also navigate public transport, often with limited information, or unfamiliar road systems.

Lastly, an important part of a holiday is sharing that holiday with others who are at home. Although the tourist fascination with taking photos or videos has been often criticised, it displays how visitors are not isolated individuals but are part of a social group. Tourists record and represent experiences in the form of photos and stories, to remind themselves of the visit and to share with others after they return home. This is a valuable part of tourism. The most successful tourist technology is the camera, specifically designed for this 'taking the visit back home'. The popularity of Internet cafés for tourists also suggests that email sent back home is becoming a significant part of the tourist experience.

Solutions

These 'problems' are not a negative part of tourism. Travelling and finding out where to go is part of the very enjoyment of tourism. Tourism transforms what might seem mundane activities into something enjoyable or even romantic. Train journeys, for example, are a common resource for the travel writer, and bus and underground travel can have their own pleasures (such as the smell of the train's tires in the Parisian metro, or the electronic sounds of the Tokyo subway). Particularly in city visits, walking between places is an important part of being in a place, with 'street life' being one of the easiest ways to access the natural life of locals .

These pleasures are a whimsical yet crucial part of the enjoyment of tourism. So, in solving these problems tourists are not simply looking for some optimal solution. Instead, solving these problems is part of the enjoyment of the experience; finding a nice café or reading a map, for example, is enjoyable in itself. Accordingly, the solutions that tourists have to these problems are often finely tuned to both the problem and the enjoyment of working through the problem.

One method that tourists use to solve their problems is sharing the visit with other tourists. Tourism is very much a social activity. A tourist generally travels with others, e.g. as part of a family group, and statistics from the US show that 79% of leisure visits involve groups of two or more. Since leisure travel is predominantly group-based, there is considerable intra-group interaction and collaboration. For example, two tourists who have just arrived at Edinburgh's main train station. The first tourist holds an "A to Z" street guide to Edinburgh, and is looking through it. While the second tourist glances around the railway station, the first tourist finds the correct page of the map. Then the second tourist takes out her glasses to look at the map, glances at the map and then points at an exit sign in the train station that names the street to which the exit leads. They then give the street guide a last look, pick up their bags and leave the station.

Even in this simple excerpt one can see a division of labour between the two tourists. The second tourist looks around the station to find the exit, while the first tourist tries to find the correct page on the map. She holds the map so as to make both the map and her progress in using it available to her companion. On finding the station, she describes the location of the station to her friend, and the friend adds the name of the street reached via the exit. With these two items of information, they now know where they are on the map, where the exit will take them and how to proceed to their destination. Reading the map is done here in such a way that it can be 'checked' by the first tourist's companion. If she makes a mistake (which is easy to do), or if they later find themselves lost, the companion can intervene. The job of remembering the route is thus shared by the two tourists. Together they use the environment to move between the map and a course of activity. The sign in the station is used to link the map with where the station exit leads.

Along with these collaborative advantages of working together, visiting with others is not without its own overheads. With the collaborative 'working out' in this clip there is also an implicit negotiation going on. The two tourists are deciding what they are going to do as well as how. Visiting with others involves considerable co-ordination in this way. The desire to visit different attractions, or simply to see different museum exhibits, means that tourist groups often split up and then need to co-ordinate getting back together. This can present considerable challenges since tourists are highly mobile. It is in these situations that mobile phones become a useful tool, in that calls can be made between individuals or sub-groups.

A more local form of this co-ordination problem also takes place in particular sites where individuals go to different rooms, or different exhibits, and they need to locate their travelling companions. This is particularly the case for tourists with children, since children sometimes run off, and must be carefully watched to see that they come to no harm. In the incidents, mothers spent considerable time shepherding children around museums, in particular, collecting all the children together before leaving the museum. For these parents a large part of their holiday was 'managing' the group and making sure that nobody got lost.

A second way in which visits are shared is through meeting other tourists. The standard jokes about holiday romances displays something of the way that meeting other people is an integral part of many tourist experiences. In part, these opportunities come from the lowered barriers to social contact. Individuals are 'on holiday' from many of their home commitments. The facilities that tourists use, such as hostels, trains and buses, also can also afford social contact. One reason behind these social contacts, and certainly a common conversation topic, is the exchange of stories and advice on where to go and what to visit.

A second way tourists solve their problems is the use of published information. The two most quintessential tourist publications are the guidebook and the map. These are often used in combination when tourists navigate and find out about what to do in different places and how to get between them. While both have been subject to computerisation, this has had only limited success. Guidebooks come in many different forms, from free handouts to Michelin and Baedeker guides. One reason why guidebooks are so useful to tourists is that they catalogue, in a structured and relatively standardised form, relevant aspects of the places that tourists visit. They list accommodation (with phone numbers), attractions (with opening times), recommended bars and restaurants, and so on. This standardisation can make strange places feel considerably safer to tourists by reducing their uncertainty.

Guidebooks also offer short 'guides to action', highlighting differences in everyday activities that might cause embarrassment. In use, however, this information needs considerable interpretation-guidebooks need to be 'put in their place'. What the guidebook says has to be combined with other information, in particular information on maps, or advice from locals. The tourists holding a map and a guidebook, and using these in combination. In particular, guidebooks were collaborative artefacts, conversation would take place around the guidebook with tourists pointing at the guidebook, and then pointing either at a map or in a direction, so as to link together the establishments being discussed with their position.

The tourists go through a number of descriptions of where the house is and what it is like to help them find it with eventually the age helping them to find the house "its probably the old one". These descriptions help the tourists to find the house, along with informing them about what they are visiting. Even with a map, a guidebook, and the assistance of a local, the tourists need to work the guidebook to 'place' the old house on the street they are actually on, and overcome some of the confusions of streets which change name, the difference between how a street is named on a map and a name that locals use. In designing technologies for tourism we should also pay attention to a second aspect of guidebooks: their physical form.

Maps have of course been a well-researched artefact in fields as widespread as cognitive psychology and cultural studies. The specific topic of way-finding has been explored in depth. One finding from these studies is that map users are significantly better at tasks that involve configuration information (such as how far one landmark is from another) than those without maps, sometimes better even than local people with years of knowledge of a place. However, perhaps surprisingly, there is little work that has examined the in-situ, non-experimental use of maps. Alternatively, tourists used maps to go towards a specific type of attraction, such as a café, but with no specific café in mind-they would head towards a street where they thought there would be cafés.

Tourists also often only had a rough idea of where they were, and would use a map to locate or orient themselves so as to head in a 'roughly correct' direction, rather than along a specific route. So, in using a map, tourists might not know where they were, might have little idea about their orientation, might not know where they were going, and might even be unsure about what they were looking for. So, map use is often less about explicit route planning and more about wandering a city in a 'roughly correct' manner. The routes that tourists used were more directional than specific, with tourists frequently stopping en route, using the map to find the direction to walk in, and then setting off again. A second feature of map use is their combination with guidebooks. A key aspect of this is how tourists combine characteristics and geography in an attempt to simultaneously solve the problems of where things are and what things there are.

As any frequent traveller will know, one of the most effective ways to find a restaurant in an unfamiliar city is to simply wander around a central area. Although by no means a perfect way of finding particular amenities, walking around exploits the tendency of certain facilities (such as bars and restaurants) to be clustered in particular area. In this way, one can also judge establishments by their appearance and menu, as one walks past. These 'clusters' are exploited in tourists' use of maps. When choosing where to go to, it is often safer to pick an area with more than one potential facility. By combining maps and guidebooks, tourists can look for 'clusters' of facilities in particular areas and go towards these particular areas rather than (or in addition to) heading towards a specific establishment.

A tourist has to link between the map and what they see of streets and landmarks. Many tourists pointing or turning their bodies towards different places to help them work out where to go. Even though the places that these tourists were going to were not visible, they turned so as to see where they were going. Indeed, when staff in the tourist information centre gave directions, they combined two different methods. One set of directions was given by drawing a line on a map-a portable and abstract version that can be used by a tourist to find their destination. Staff combined this with 'showing' in physical space where the destination was and how to get there: saying "it's behind us on Argyle Street" while using an arm movement to point in a specific direction. A last point about maps' use concerns how they are frequently read in advance of getting to the place the map describes. This was a common use of maps.

Indeed, this pointed towards a much-neglected aspect of using maps: their educational function. A major aim of using a map is to learn about a place sufficiently that one can get around without using a map, learning about a place by looking at where the streets go, the names of the streets and potential landmarks.

One tourist who spent over twenty minutes at a Glasgow train station reading a map of a popular mountain walk. In looking at the map, this tourist was learning about his walk. While not explicitly finding his way, he was learning about things that would help him when on the walk, such as the distances between places and what landmarks and sights there are around the area. When tourists use maps in situ by the process of travelling around, they are also learning about sites and streets in such a way that if they return they will have more idea of the location and how to get around.

Pre-visiting and Post-visiting

Tourists pre-visit a place by reading about it before they go there. Through arranging information and reading about a place before travelling, a tourist can do some of the organising activity for the holiday before the holiday. As with many of the other solutions outlined above, previsiting is not only practical; it is enjoyable. It extends the excitement of the holiday and builds anticipation as well as giving the visitor some sort of idea of what they are visiting before they get there.

Pre-visiting also happens while on the holiday itself, with tourists gathering information about places and planning what they are going to do. One important aspect of tourist planning is that it is 'satisficing', in that plans are 'good enough' rather than detailed plans of activity. Indeed, tourists' plans are often deliberately ambiguous so that they can take into account future contingencies. As Suchman argues, plans often do not determine behaviour but rather are used flexibly in deciding what to do. This acknowledges that decisions are often easier to make when one is actually in a particular place. For example, when planning a route, planning the complete route in advance using a map is often quite difficult. An alternative approach is to plan an ambiguous route in advance, and then picking specific roads by using road signs when one is driving.

In this way, tourist plans are often deliberately designed to be only as specific as necessary. A number of the tourists talked about allocating days to particular places before they travelled. This sort of planning leaves a lot unspecified: when each day is, and what activities are done in each place, for example. Yet this sort of planning acknowledges that these sort of details are better kept flexible until closer to the time, as they will be dependent on local transport details, and can be adjusted in the face of other local contingencies, such as changing weather. Indeed, a stereotypical bad holiday is one that is excessively planned, in that changing circumstances are not be taken into account. A second interesting aspect of tourist plans is how they follow or copy plans provided by others.

A popular example of this is the package holiday, but even on package holidays not all of one's time is structured: many activities (such as choosing a restaurant) still involve some planning during the visit. The tours thus provided information and structure about the city, as much as being a strict plans or activity to follow in themselves. If pre-visiting is about planning, then post-visiting is about reminiscing and sharing. Tourists often get together in groups to talk through their holidays, or to talk about their holidays to others who were not there. Photographs are very important for this activity in that they provide a framework around which stories can be told and experiences shared. Talking through the visit with photographs can take place both with those who were present on holiday and those who were not; in one form it is reminiscence, in another it allows the holiday to be shared. The combination of talk and interaction around pictures supports both these activities.

Post-visiting is thus a powerful way of extending the enjoyment of a tourist visit out beyond the visit itself. It also acts as a recommendation mechanism for different places - it allowing us to see 'what places are like' through our friends, and outside the commercially produced views of brochures and television. Indeed, some tourists who are on longer holidays go to the point of creating rich travelogues of their holiday, involving photographs, videos and text that are brought together to tell the story of their holiday. These travelogues usually exist in the form of photo albums, although a number of travelogues do exist on the Internet. However, there are considerable barriers to creating travelogues online-crafting web pages can take considerable time, and access to a PC and the Internet can be difficult while on holiday.

Barriers to New Technologies

Although tourism presents a number of barriers to introducing new technology - in particular the need for devices to be sufficiently mobile—tourists have already adopted many new technologies, e.g. the web, mobile phones and digital cameras. This suggests that there are opportunities for new tourist systems that fit tourist practice. An important part of tourism is sharing the visit with others. One problem that tourists face is co-ordinating their activities while they are separated-in particular getting groups back together again. One application that would assist this is a handheld or phone-based system that allowed tourists to communicate their locations to each other. So, if a group splits into two, they could choose to 'tie' their locations together so that each subgroup would be able to see where the other was. 'Tying' in this way could support synchronous awareness without running into difficult privacy problems.

In addition, technology could support tourists showing the routes they took and things they did when they meet up again. This could allow them to make recommendations to their companions and also to other tourists whom they meet. A second aspect of sharing visits is collaboration between tourists who do not know each other. One recommendation here is for technology to support sharing comments and reviews on different tourist attractions. However, it is important here to make this an interactive experience between tourists; exchange of information is as much about meeting other tourists as it is exchanging information. This could be supported by using public machines or message walls where tourists can meet as they exchange information, or by enhancing existing sights where tourists meet, such as on city tours.

As discussed above, electronic guidebooks and maps have been a popular application area for mobile technology, with existing system generally following a similar format to paper guidebooks, augmented with GPS. One innovation that electronic guidebooks could support is in making connections between where attractions are and what they are. Electronic guidebooks should explicitly support the comparison of information, allowing users to quickly move between related pieces of information. Partly due to the limited screen size, mobile systems seldom offer this feature. Pocket Internet Explorer, for example, only allows the user to load one web page at a time. One solution to this could be paper maps and electronic guidebooks that are designed to be used together. This would remove some of the disadvantages of the small screen by allowing users to juxtapose the PDA and the map in their visual field. More direct coupling is also feasible, e.g. through the PDA's sensing of printed glyphs and barcodes.

Mapping systems could also support more of the 'wandering' behaviour of tourists; for example, showing at a glance whether a tourist is going in the right direction rather than simply supporting a pre-determined route. Indicators could show nearby attractions, cafés, areas or main streets to support serendipitous discovery. This sort of representation moves beyond supporting wayfinding to supporting the broader range of tasks that tourists undertake when navigating. So, such a representation would support going between one shopping district and another, while looking for a café. In cases like this it is not the exact route that is important, although walking in the right direction is important, but a more general sense of learning about the city as one wanders around. Maps themselves could also show more of the 'social zoning' of different places, such as what areas are good for shopping, going out, or eating.

Distinct from guidebooks, electronic tour guide systems attempt to offer information about a visitor's current location, and suggestions of where they might want to go next. These systems, such as the Lancaster GUIDE system, and more recently the EU funded "m-toGuide" system, have generally been based around a 'walk-up pop-up' model where information (voice and text) is pushed at users based on their current location.

Presenting information to tourists while they are actually at an attraction may have limited utility, since at that point the environment is likely to contain richer sources of information than can be provided by a PDA. Tours instead act as structures through which tourists can learn about the place being visited, and can use to build their own, more ad hoc plans. Systems should therefore present tours and attractions to tourists in such a way as to allow them to browse and learn from the tours rather than strictly following them, and to be aware of 'official' tourist attractions without being restricted to them. Viewing tours in advance would allow tourists to 'pre-visit' and judge different places and make their own plans about what to do rather than only following an official tour.

Lastly, the importance of post-visiting for tourists, allowing them to communicate and discuss their visit when they got home. The 'travelblog' system allows tourists to build web-based travelogues describing their travels. These entries consist of pictures, videos and text captured on a Nokia 7650 camera-phone. These entries are then emailed from the phone to a server that automatically builds a web log combining the images and text. While some travelblogs are already on the Internet, created through increasingly popular weblogging software, the system also supports users replying to entries and having these messages forwarded via SMS to the tourist. Although this mechanism is very simple, it supports travellers updating their travelblog from anywhere in the world and extends the value of weblogs to the travelling tourist.

Hospitality Technology Architecture

The hospitality industry is in the unenviable position of having to meet guest needs, owner/franchisee demands and employee expectations -all in the face of threats of terrorism, war and economic uncertainties. Guests seek differentiated experiences. Owners seek more timely access to information. Employees seek improvements in guestfacing applications. Yet, most guest-facing technologies do not contain the functionality and integration necessary to support service excellence. They simply have not kept up with the changing demands.

The industry is struggling with a single source of the truth and single image strategies for inventory, guest information and marketing/operational content. This perspective on the evolution of technology in the hospitality industry advocates a centrally or regionally provisioned architecture to develop an above-property view of strategic property and guestspecific applications.

Key Challenges

Hoteliers are forced to simultaneously focus in different directions. Their reactions to these challenges and how effective they are at juggling these factors will ultimately define how well they weather the storm. Key challenges include:

— *Commoditization* : Brand capital is eroding and hotels are threatened by commoditization. Guests are becoming savvier-they seek differentiated experiences. The brand is no longer the driving force...increasingly more and more guests are becoming brand agnostic-their perception of limited brand differentiation further exasperates the issue. Guests are increasingly looking for niche offerings and personalized services that are delivered consistently.

— *Distribution* : Relentless rate pressure brought on by rate transparency, online intermediaries and aggressive corporate procurement tactics are compounding the issue. Online intermediaries are driving a wedge between major brands and the brand-agnostic guest. These online channels are often popular with hotel owners who see them as an effective way to move inventory. Some hoteliers are combating this by pushing direct connect strategies to combat the effect in the corporate market, reducing the dependency on the global distribution systems and enabling a one-to-one relationship with the guest.

— *Owner/Franchisee Relations* : Owners and franchisees seek greater transparency. They want better services from their franchisors. They seek access to operational information in near-real time, giving them a clear picture of how their portfolios are performing. They want a clear indication why they should align themselves with company A vs.company B.

— *Front Line Demands* : There is greater pressure from employees to deliver service excellence, but preparation and training are limited. Employees seek the tools and technologies that are built around the tenet of service excellence-as front line deliverers of service, they seek assistance in meeting and exceeding guest expectations. Unfortunately, systems have not always been built on this principle.

Hotels should differentiate their product through differentiated experiences-transitioning from a focus on the product or destination to a focus on a personalized end-to-end guest experience. They must also respond to changing consumer dynamics by emphasizing niche products and services. Compelling points of difference that make one hotel stand out from another should be identified and marketed.

Next Generation Technology Architecture

The industry will rely heavily on a next generation technology architecture to address the challenges hotels are facing at present. This architecture will provide the underlying infrastructure and services that allow hotels to reposition their employees to focus on value-added guest interactions, by automating core transactions and providing consistent access to guest data. It will provide hotels with opportunities to leverage technology advances to improve the guest experience. Technology will be pervasive yet invisible.

Hotels will have the ability to quickly and flexibly innovate and react to market needs, wants and desires. New concept time-to-market will be greatly reduced, aided by adaptive technology. Hotels will standardize back-of-the-house and key front-of-thehouse functions across business units, brands, regions and properties, by placing them on a single technology platform and implementing a common business process and organizational framework. External linkages will become easier-applications will draw on common standards libraries for information interchange among systems. Complicated, customized interfaces between systems and organizations will be passé. The operational and financial benefits will be enormous-cross-brand employee mobility and training cost reduction are some advantages.

A logical move for agile hotel corporations, next generation technology applications will be based around an on-demand technology infrastructure. IT services, applications and data will be available as and when needed. Hotel companies will be able to provide transactional-based models to their franchisees, owners and individual properties, which will only pay for services availed. Installing applications will involve downloading and running them within a browser window. Hotels will move to a variable cost structure where financial models are based on a per-use concept. Supporting and managing infrastructure that is not fully utilized will be a thing of the past. This will free up much needed capital which hotels can use to focus on their raison d'etre.

Hospitality Technology Model

The new hospitality technology model will place a greater emphasis on enterprise-wide standards. It will employ adaptable, reusable components that can plug into each other-applications will be easily configurable depending upon business size and scope. This new model will be based around a single image of guest information, inventory and content. Users will see the same data regardless of where they tap into the value chain. Hotels will regain control of distribution by limiting the use of indirect online channels; direct connect strategies in the corporate market will become the norm, rather than the exception.

Application services will be delivered above-property via on-demand solutions. They would include property management, point of sale, sales and catering, HR, back office and financials, resulting in improved services and a reduced technology footprint on property. Advances in network connectivity, reliability and security will allow these applications to be hosted centrally and made available through a browser-based front end. Where connectivity is an issue, local models will be supported-relevant data will be downloaded, used to support business processes, and synched with the central repository the next time network connectivity is made available.

The next generation hospitality technology architecture will bring tremendous benefit to the hospitality industry. An on-demand, aboveproperty delivery of services will reduce IT costs and infrastructure investment at the property level. Standardized applications and a single image of guests, inventory and content will provide a consistent view across all touch points in the value chain. Linkages with external applications and organizations will be handled via common information interchange standards. Hotel management will have access to a common, centralized view of pertinent operational information that will be made available to them via customizable on-demand workplaces.

6

Risk Management in Hospitality

According to the Travel Industry Association and the World Tourism Organization, in the coming decades event managers can expect to see greater numbers of people traveling to concerts, conventions, meetings, and sports activities. The growth of the leisure industry will increase risk, and the need to manage that risk is becoming an ever-greater challenge to the entire tourism/leisure industry. Before we can even begin to examine some of the issues in managing risk, it is essential to review how leisure time is changing in the United States. Over the last decade, scholars have noted that leisure time has taken on the following characteristics:

a) Shorter vacation periods

b) Competition determined not by distance but by cost of travel to destination

c) Greater access to information due to the Internet and the World Wide Web

d) Greater exchange of "word of mouth" information between people who have never met each other

e) New opportunities for cybercriminals

Both in developed and in emerging nations, risk managers in tourism and travel, and meetings and events must face and seek ways to confront crises prior to their occurrence.

Risks to the events and tourism industries may come in many forms. Some of these risks are due to issues of potential violence, health and safety concerns, or unique and unexpected weather events such as floods, droughts, and hurricanes/typhoons.

Principles of Risk Management

These basic theoretical principles form the foundation for why risk management is so important to every aspect of the tourism industry from attractions to events, from hotels to meetings.

— Events and meetings are a form of tourism and thus suffer from the same sociological phenomena as tourism.

— Events and meetings often follow the same patterns, be they mega-events, or mini-events.

— Whenever an act of violence occurs within the world of events or meetings, the media are almost certain to report it, forcing the local event industry to be embroiled in acts of crisis management.

— Perceptions about an event crisis tend to be almost as devastating as the crisis itself.

— The farther away one is from a crisis location, the worse the crisis will appear to be and the longer the crisis will remain in the collective travel subconscious.

"Crises in the tourism industry can take many shapes and forms: from terrorism to sexual harassment, white collar crime to civil disturbance, a jet crashing into a hotel to cash flow problems, guest injury to strikes, bribery to price fixing, noise to vandalism, guest misuse of facilities to technology change ."

Whether they are natural or man-made crises,"there is no doubt that the travel and tourism industry is especially susceptible and vulnerable to crisis." Furthermore, "Tourism is often unable to rebound as quickly as other businesses, since much of a destination's attraction is derived from its image". The risk of these crises is the very social cancer that can eat away at the events industry. Postmodern tourism is often driven by events and therefore the industry must improve its risk management practices to destroy this potential disease.

The age of instant communication via satellite television and computers means that there is now selective knowledge and ignorance. Never have individuals around the world had greater access to information and never has there been greater levels of "information overload." What this plethora of information means is that we now have more information on how to handle risks and to prevent crises, and that the consequences of failure can be more devastating than ever before. To begin our understanding of the role of risk management in the event and tourism industries, it is important that we review some of the historical perspectives that have shaped the role of risk management in the world of events and tourism. Historically oriented sociologists have observed the similarities that link the end of the nineteenth century to the end of the twentieth century.

Event risk managers, then, must work in a world that can be very confusing as well as trying. To confound matters, postmodern scholars point to the blurring of sociological categories in the daily lives of people living in the developed countries:Postmodernist vacations are usually stressful; there are few exotic places left in the world, and most vacation spots promise to deliver the same bland product-fun. one could just as well spend one's time in a shopping mall. In fact, shopping frequently becomes the primary activity in postmodernist vacations.

Some of the major differences between life at the end of the nineteenth century and life at the end of the twentieth century indicate that we not only classify leisure in different ways, but that the risks involved in the pursuit of leisure have changed. The first envisioned the democratization of leisure and consumption; the second the democratization of work. If culture was a function of affluence and leisure, then universal abundance . . . held out the best hope of cultural democracy. Leisure is no longer viewed as simply idle time for the rich. Indeed, a simple list of some of the ways that we spend our leisure time would surprise our grandparents and great-grandparents. Following is a list of some of the events that occupy our time:

a) Family and human life cycle events, such as weddings, family reunions, and barbecues
b) Community events, such as school picnics, business outings, and holiday celebrations
c) Organized shopping exhibitions
d) Civil and political events
e) Business meetings and conferences
f) Sports events, ranging from Little League to the Olympic Games
g) Concerts
h) Religious gatherings and pilgrimages
i) Local and national political gatherings
j) Fairs and festivals

The preceding list demonstrates one of the major problems of risk management in the meetings and events industry. In the modern world, there is a great deal of spillover from a leisure activity to a business activity. Classical nineteenth-century authors of leisure enjoyed clear distinctions between leisure and work. In the twenty-first century, these distinctions no longer exist. One example is the major religious pilgrimage known as the hajj. On this journey, millions of Muslims travel to Mecca.

How do we classify this event? Is it tourism, travel, business, or convention? Certainly all of the risks that are inherent in the other four entities mentioned are also part of the hajj. From the moment the traveler sets out for Mecca, he or she is subject to risk, be it in the form of clean water, sleeping facilities, safe travel, or crowd control. This spillover from one field to another is called "dedifferentiation." In today's modern world, it is hard to dedifferentiate between what was once a simple family gathering and what is today a small convention.

Today's mobile society has a very different view of leisure from that of past societies. "Leisure for them [us] closely resembles work, since much of it consists of strenuous and for the most part solitary exercise. Even shopping, their ruling passion, takes on the character of a grueling ordeal: 'Shop till you drop!' ". This dedifferentiation between work and play, as exemplified by the shop/drop syndrome, is one of the theoretical underpinnings to the understanding of risk management.

"Postmodernism problematises the distinction between representations and reality . . . or what Baudrillard famously argues, what we increasingly consume are signs or representations". Risk management's job, then, is to keep substance from forming into the basis of a crisis, and if such a crisis should occur to contain its secondary effects. The onset of the information age in the twentieth century has closely paralleled the growth of the travel and tourism industry. Mass tourism is a phenomenon of the twentieth century. It was only with the end of World War II that travel, like so many products, entered the modern world of mass production. This success story also contains within it the seeds of crises.

With millions of people traveling daily, and with the onset of the information age, word-of-mouth/computer information spreads rapidly, diseases are carried from one nation to the next, and the potential for violent cross-fertilization, both in ideas and actions, becomes ubiquitous. For example, throughout the world, tourists have been inundated with accounts of widespread acts of violence: in schools, in the workplace, and on public highways. The spread of information, both in written and in pictorial form, has never been so ever present. For example, television and radio broadcast events as they unfold, and the Web permits word-of-mouth dialogue in computerized form to spread instantaneously.

Furthermore, the use of e-mail has transformed the world into an electronic village. All this rapid interchange among people makes the life of the event risk manager even more difficult as even small events can become large crises. Today's event guest is aware of violence not only in urban centers around the world but even in rural areas, be they in Uganda or in the United States. This vast sea of information means that event guests have greater access to information and that the events industry has less ability to hide information. What is still unknown is at what point an excess of information may cause guests simply to shut down and undergo a rejection process. Leisureoriented risk management specialists face the irony that, as information spreads, it increases the potential for violent behavior.

Risk managers, must deal with an industry that not only is an integral part of many nations' economies, but also plays a major role in the disbursement of information. It is an industry that produces and is produced by information, an industry that sells reality and education, while creating its own postmodern realities based on simulata and plausible facts. In such a diverse industry as the events industry, it is not surprising that there is no one single unifying theory of event risk management.

This is a multifaceted industry that has yet to be defined: Are event attendees the product or the consumers of the product? Is the industry composed of tangibles or is it an intangible many-headed hydra that no one can quite tame? The events industry encompasses such diverse individuals as business travelers, people passing through a locale, people visiting family and friends, delegates to conferences and conventions, audience members, and pleasure seekers.

Post-tourist (modren tourist) is stimulated by the interpenetration or the collision between different facets and representations of the tourism sight. The accessories of the sight-the gift shops, the eating places, the tourist coaches and other tourists-are celebrated for being as much a key part of the tourist experience as the sight itself. Many event professionals, however, tend to divide the industry into two broad groupings: movement for pleasure and movement for work.

Vacations or leisure events traditionally have been a means by which people attempted to escape from the stress and rigors of everyday life. What once served, however, as a way to repair body and soul has now become a new area for victimization, and that victimization often forms the basis of the job of the risk manager in the prevention of crises. The perception that pleasure travel to a particular location may result in the visitor's bodily harm, loss of property, or even death can destroy that locale's tourism industry or the reputation of an event. Riots at rock concerts and European football (soccer) matches, highly publicized acts of crime in Mexico, terrorist acts against tourists in Egypt, Yemen, and East Africa have all caused a major loss in revenue.

These risks turned into reality serve to remind travel/ visitor officials of just how sensitive their industry is to security issues. These "crises" often force two components of a nation's society, the travel/events industry and the security industry, to interact with each other and to learn just how interdependent they are on one another. Questions of violence directly impact these industries' ability to promote a safe and worry-free experience. Vacationers, viewing their trips as an escape from their personal problems and those of the world, tend to assume that they are safe from crime, disease, and even natural calamities.

Business travelers, being more cognizant of safety issues, may also shy away from high-risk locales. Although no locale can provide a perfect security/safety environment, an understanding of some of the sociological theoretical models under which visitors operate can help the student of event risk management to prepare for, deal with, and recover from moments of crises. An unlimited wealth of data demonstrates that the travel and events industries cannot tolerate an environment that is perceived to be unstable.

City, county, state/provincial, and national law enforcement agencies play a vital role in making tourists and event attendees feel safe. Convention and visitor bureaus (CVBs), resort hotels, convention organizers, and event planners are aware that a pleasure visitor need not come to their particular community, conference, or event, and therefore see any attack against the safety or security of their guests to be an attack against the essence of their industry. For example, high crime rates, especially at night, do more than just keep visitors and locals alike from frequenting downtown establishments. These crime rates produce a sociological cancerous blight that in the end gnaws away not only at the tourism industry, but at the chance for holding a particular event, eventually destroying it from the inside.

To make matters even more difficult for the event risk management professional, many security forces have only a superficial knowledge of event tourism and travel practices and theory. Few police departments are cognizant that, taken together, the travel and events industry is the world's largest industry or of the relationship between travel and their own community's economic well-being. There are several exceptions to this rule. To illustrate this point, let us examine one city, Anaheim, California. Anaheim has created a special police unit, called Tourism Oriented Policing Services (TOPS), to deal with almost every travel, meeting, and/or convention problem imaginable. A special Anaheim police unit now works with Disneyland and its convention center, focusing on the unique risks involved with conventions and travel.

Some of the risks that this unit has learned to handle are risks to non-English-speaking guests, robberies at local hotels, specific crimes targeted at the convention market (such as the stealing of laptop computers), and the special risks that take place in valet companies serving the events industry. In other words, tourismoriented policing is not just crime fighting but also understanding the risks that event-goers face and developing ways to manage those risks. Police and other security personnel are often geared to the ideal of "to protect" rather than the marketing ideal of "to serve."

The TOPS philosophy changes this equation and declares success not as "How many crimes did we solve?" but rather as "How many risks did we identify and how many crimes did we therefore prevent?" TOPS hopes to change the role of law enforcement agencies by helping them to understand how the events industry impacts a community: what its role is in gaining often needed foreign currency, creating employment opportunities, or improving a community's public image and perception of itself. Additionally, many of the attributes that attract visitors to a community also add to that community's uniqueness and quality of life.

Because tourism and events are nontangible products-a "feeling" rather than a "thing"-risk management is dependent not only on concrete plans but also on attitudes held by both the risk management professional and the public. Xenophobic attitudes or simply a "take the guest for granted attitude" are felt by the industry's clients who react negatively to such attitudes, be that person an employee or simply a citizen of the locale being visited. The risk management professional's attitude is therefore a critical element to his or her success. If these professionals resent their guests and view them as intruders, then no amount of fancy marketing will undo the economic damage done to that community's tourism or events industry.

Because risk management, from the guest's perspective, touches so many aspects of his or her life away from home, the potential for a crisis is ever present. Danger can occur not only at the event itself, but also in restaurants and places of entertainment that are in close proximity to an event site, hotels, and transportation arteries. This lack of definition means that event risk management, in its broadest scope, like the industry itself, is undefined. Like a one-cell animal, risk management grows, splits, and travels throughout the social system.

Sociological Theories

Functionalists understand the social system as a series of interlocking components. They assume that a change in any one component of a social system will produce changes throughout the system. From the perspective of event risk management, then, a problem/crisis in any one part of the industry is bound to create problems for that locale's entire industry. Due to this interlocking, functionalists do not distinguish safety issues from security issues. Functionalists argue instead that any problem that touches upon the well-being of the guest (and therefore the locale's industry as a whole) is one and the same, and any distinction between these two sides of the same coin is mere academic sophistry.

A functionalist noted: "Increasingly vicious acts of terrorism against tourists and tourist destinations, rising international alarm over traveler health [and] safety, and the growing economic competitiveness of safe, hygienic, and environmentally sensitive or "green" tourism will be relentless drivers". Functionalists argue that, from the perspective of the tourist, a safety issue and a security issue are interchangeable. The functionalist perspective is an important tool in our understanding of the interlinkage of tourism components. What functionalists fail to measure, however, is the intensity of the crisis.

While functionalist theory sends up a red flag and warns the risk manager that the potential for a crisis is developing, it fails to provide an accurate forecast about the crisis's severity. Functionalism cannot tell the risk manager what parts of the system will be most affected and what the crisis's time frame is or who in a particular crisis may come out to be the winner or the loser. Thus, a murder in a hotel may also affect restaurant business, but the tourism scholar does not know how deep the effect will be or how long it will take to become a crisis.

A second classical way of looking at a tourism risk management system is through conflict theory. Conflict theorists assume that any social system or component-driven industry has a high potential for conflict/competition, not only between locales but also within locales. For example, a city wants to bring in more conventions. A number of businesses, hotels, restaurants, and nightspots, would be highly supportive of such a decision. Nevertheless, opposition arises from locals who fear greater competition for parking space, higher road usage, and an increasing number of social problems.

In such a scenario, the events industry might find itself in direct competition with any number of coalitions that band together to limit the number of conventions brought into the city. In conflict theory, there are always winners and losers and tourism/events are seen as a "zero-sum game." From this perspective, locations and events compete for space, publicity, and clientele. This competition, in turn, is one of the reasons for the business life cycle. Thus, a tourism or event crisis in one part of the world may be seen as an opportunity in another part of the world.

The history of consumer products has shown that survival may not be based on quality of product but rather on quality of marketing, timing, or symbiotic name recognition. Tourism crises may cause a shakedown in the tourism market and produce strong marketing agencies, but these crises do not necessarily translate into a better tourism product or a better managed event. The prism of symbolic interaction is another way by which to analyze a tourism crisis. Over the years, this perspective, as first understood by a sociologist has evolved into postmodernism and then into iconic theory. Scholars who accept this form of theoretical paradigm argue that tourism, meetings, or special events are highly sensitive to image creation.

The basis for their academic argument is that these industries sell memories and are "image" producers. The meetings and events industry, for those who work in symbolic interaction, is about the packaging of a collective memory and associating it with (a) specific place(s) in time or space. From the symbolic interaction perspective, crises are interpreted in a symbolic and symbiotic manner. An example of this symbolism is in the presence or nonpresence of a police/security force at an event site. In many event venues, a police/security presence may serve the industry as a "psychological" security blanket and a way to avoid crises. Visitors report that they feel more comfortable when they know that an area is well patrolled.

In contrast, however, too many police officers in a particular location may send the message that there is a good reason to be afraid, that the officers are there as a result of a crisis, or that the area is dangerous. Because most people connect a uniformed officer to a range of meanings, the tourism center that chooses to have a security force present must create a setting in which these security personnel symbolize hospitality rather than restraint, service over protection, and security over threat.

When security departments produce negative images, they can become part of the risk crisis. For example, negative media reports about Los Angeles and Mexico City have added additional challenges to the tourism industries in those cities. The recent example of New York City police officers doing nothing while more than fifty women were molested in Central Park during the Puerto Rico Day parade has been reported throughout the world. In that case, due to poor risk management and assessment, a major crisis developed for both the city's tourism community and its police force.

The opposite can also be true. In some communities, local security forces have succeeded in becoming symbolic icons, representing not just the use of force but also a cultural attraction. In those cases, the police force is not only a deterrent to crime but also an important icon of that society. The aforementioned classical sociological theories:

a) Events are a volunteeristic activity: As such, the industry must resell itself on a consistent basis. The theoretical consequences of this proposition are many.

b) Most guests do not distinguish between the concepts of safety and security: The poisoning of food and an act of terrorism often have the same consequences. This dedifferentiation between the terms again holds a number of consequences for the industry.

c) There is no one formula to describe all guests. What may be a crisis for one person may not be a crisis for another person. Classical psychographic tourism theory tends to divide visitors along various continuums.

During the last century, all forms of event participation have grown from an activity of the well-to-do to a part of everyday life. Leisure, parasitic in nature, was once the idle time of the rich. In the mid-twentieth century, leisure became a product for the working person, and once it became producible en masse, it became an integral part of local economies. There are several other theoretical models that can be of use to the event risk manager. George Ritzer discusses the McDonaldization of much of the world. This thesis holds that service-oriented businesses have undergone a paradigm shift. Ritzer offers the following postulates:

a) Service industries, such as restaurants and hotels, have become rationalized to the point that efficiency over service has become the goal. Risk, then, is an issue of efficiency. Where efficiency ceases, crises begin. Even the wasting of time is a risk that can become a crisis. To understand Ritzer's position, one only need observe the rage that takes place whenever a flight is delayed or canceled or there is a traffic jam on a busy interstate highway.

b) Service industries must be measured in quantifiable terms. Ritzer argues that customers want to know exactly how much a vacation or event will cost. Crises may occur, then, in cases where there are cost overruns or missed places on stated itineraries.

c) Service industries are seeking scripted experiences. Disney may be the best example of the scripted, or predictable, experience, though cruises also follow this pattern. Vacations, according to Ritzer's theory, enter into a period of crisis when, on a meta level, they cease to be similar to our daily lives. In other words, even what is different becomes the same in that we "script" the differences into our play.

d) Service personnel are being replaced by nonhuman apparatus. Ritzer argues that the machine is slowly replacing the human. In risk management, for example, there is the use of security cameras instead of human service agents. This dehumanization of tourism means that crises develop when machines break. The breakage leads to irrationalization due to the fact that it becomes almost impossible to speak to a human being. An example of such irrationalization is the attempt to find a human being in the maze of voice mail after a crisis has occurred at an event.

e) As the tourism/event industry becomes more rationalized, Ritzer argues, in the best Hegelian sense, an irrational element occurs. Within this model, a crisis is any irrational moment/occurrence/event within the rationalized tourist experience.

In Sternberg's terms, tourism or events are placed within a series of contexts that give the tourist or event guest's experience "added meaning". As the added meaning develops, the first, or realist, meaning becomes depleted. Thus, as Sternberg notes: "... one of the turn-of-the century's early realizations is that culture is a depletable resource. This is not because it cannot be used again and again-it certainly can; rather because through repeated use its marginal evocativeness declines". Sternberg's analysis helps to explain why so many locals see themselves in a state of crisis due to tourism's interaction with the local culture. Sternberg argues then that to manage the risk at an event, the event risk manager must prevent the risk by:

a) *Staging the product* : By this, Sternberg means that the "tourism product's safety" must be organized in such a way that it achieves its aims for both the consumer (visitor) and the supplier.

b) *Arranging the product* : Risk management must stand out within its geographical or psychological environment.

c) *Contextualizing the product* : Risk management needs to be placed within, or purposely removed from, the context of itself, be that context physical, historical, or psychological.

d) *Thematizing the product* : Sternberg challenges his readers to conceptualize how event risk management fits in with the overall theme. What expectations does it meet or not meet?

e) *Authenticizing the product* : By authenticization, Sternberg does not mean real or not real, but rather he asks if risk managers provide a genuine experience while still protecting the public.

Perhaps the greatest crisis that event management can encounter is the loss of life. Be this loss from kidnapping at a diving resort in Southeast Asia or a serial killer stalking the streets of a large urban center, no destination or venue can long survive capricious and random acts of violence. To combat this threat, event security specialists have developed techniques such as:

a) Interacting with guests as an implicit anticrime tool. Even in cities with high crime rates, crime tends to be highly concentrated in small geographic regions. Security specialists can instruct tourists on the safest routes between attractions. These interactions, however, require highly trained security professionals in tourism and tourism safety/security.

b) Developing, in conjunction with local tourism offices/ bureaus and event organizers, plans to deal with event guests who are victimized by crime. Tourism theory predicts that kind words and caring after a crime has occurred can (but do not always) mitigate some of the crime's negative effects. A security officer's professionalism can create a situation where the victimized tourist leaves with a positive, or at least less negative, attitude about the locale's hospitality rather than as a vocal critic.

c) Becoming ambassadors of goodwill for their product. Police and security departments may wish to consider the adoption of special uniforms that match their city's image. Such uniquely tailored uniforms remind local townspeople that their police department/security force not only serves and protects them, but has also adopted a proactive stance in helping to bring economic benefit to the community.

Not all crises are of a violent nature. As the range of tourism crises to manage is exhaustive, following are some other techniques that have been used:

Developing interesting jobs and creating high morale: By creating interesting and well-paying jobs, the community's stake in its local tourism industry increases. As such, when crises do happen, the entire community pulls together to help mitigate and rebuild from the crises.

Improving the quality of life : Typically, tourists and event guests visit communities with sound ecologies, good restaurants, and a multitude of attractions. These same considerations are important factors in determining a community's quality of life. By creating an atmosphere that visitors enjoy, tourism/travel officials encourage leaders in both the public and the private sectors to further improve the community's quality-of-life aspects.

Being open and honest: When a crisis occurs, the last thing the tourism industry can afford is to lie. Facts about the crisis should be given to the media in a nondefensive and forthright manner. Specific people should be designated as representatives who can provide the media with clear and precise facts.

From a tourism/travel perspective, crises have certain common patterns and "life cycles." Accordingly, the risk manager should take into account the following:

a) Determining what preparations are already in place and what resources are available.

b) Involving the local population in the disaster. Is there special attention that can be given by the locals to the survivors?

c) Considering the postdisaster healing process.

f) Knowing that no place is immune. The worst possible mindframe is for you to believe that no form of disaster can occur at your locale. For example, the random shootings of tourists that have taken place in the United States are exactly that, random. So far, there has been no pattern determined as to type of place, type of perpetrator, or type of victim.

g) Being prepared for a worst case scenario. In any disaster, there will be a threat of personal injury and death. Disasters mean that there will be disruption of operations, financial strain on the tourism locale or company, and damage to the tourism/travel company's image.

7

Pre-Acquisition Management

Acquisitions have a tremendous impact on the hotel industry industry, but there is a definite lack of comprehensive and systematic research about the underlying structure of the mergers and acquisitions (M&A) phenomenon in the hotel industry. The acquisition process itself has the most important role in determining acquisition activities and outcomes. However, to date there have been no studies that have attempted to identify the key issues that impact the processes of acquisition strategy formulation (pre-acquisition management) and acquisition strategy implementation (post-acquisition integration) in the lodging industry. Also, there have been no studies to date that have identified post-acquisition performance evaluation criteria.

Previuos studies about corporate acquisitions have attempted to discover evidence about a part of the whole acquisitions process, such as motives or objectives of acquisition, post-acquisition performance, either stock returns or operating performance, sources of shareholder wealth in corporate acquisitions, influences on post-acquisition integration, and others. These studies have investigated the corporate acquisition issues within uni-dimensional frameworks, i.e., one issue at a time. In order to pursue more rigorous and practical studies in the future, it is necessary to take an integrated and holistic viewpoint that includes the most critical corporate acquisition issues simultaneously and in a multi-dimensional framework.

Many researchers have predicted the consolidation trend of the hotel industry. According to Lattin, "Many players believe that 'big' is synonymous with 'best' and that the larger their chain, the greater the profitability of their success". Lattin also predicted that, "In the future, look for a smaller number of large chains with multiple brands and extensive distribution systems, and expect more price competition among the aging, all-purpose hotels constructed during the 1960s and '70s". An explanation of this consolidation trend can be found in the hotel industry itself, where good economics and technological and logistic developments are emphasizing the importance of size. Consolidating chains of hotels promises to take advantage of scale economies. Most importantly, many hotel acquirers have used acquisitions to obtain multiple lines of brands over the various segments.

According to Mercer Management Consulting, in the 1990s the success rate of corporate acquisitions is barely 50 percent, whereas in the 1980s, 57 percent of acquisition deals failed. Acquisition is one of the most frequently used instruments for consistent growth. According to Smith & Hershman, "A dollar earned through growth is worth 30 percent to 50 percent more than the same dollar earned through cost-cutting". Moreover, Marks & Mirvis argued that, "Increasing revenue 1 percent has five times greater impact on the bottom line than decreasing operating expenses 1 percent". Based upon this information, if firms utilized acquisitions well as a growth medium, there would be a better possibility that firms could achieve value growth through acquisitions.

Many previous studies that have been based upon a perspective of rational choice have had two key points: strategic fit and organizational fit. Some researchers have acknowledged that the rational choice perspective may not provide a thorough view of acquisition processes and outcomes. Correspondingly, Jemison and Sitkin argued that the acquisition process itself has had the crucial role in determining acquisition activities and outcomes, and the conventional choice perspective should be supplemented with a process perspective. The process perspective focuses on the idea that the acquisition process will affect the post-acquisition performance of the acquiring firm, and has a complementary relationship with traditional strategic fit and organizational fit.

According to Jemison and Sitkin, strategic fit or organizational fit approaches were focused on "successful and unsuccessful practices, and that these perspective approaches are a source of interesting research ideas. However, applied research can sometimes miss key issues that theoretical approaches reveal. Such is the case in acquisition research where clues to understanding acquisition outcomes may be discovered more readily in a variety of theories that direct to the underlying process-driven impediments to effective acquisitions".

Jemison and Sitkin stated that the process perspective is an alternative model that will replace the traditional and popular choice perspective. They pointed out that the process model is the one that emphasizes the role of the corporate acquisition process itself. They argues that the lack of systematic and thorough attention to potential problems of post-acquisition integration appears to reflect the difficulty of recognizing the process itself as part of the problem.

According to Young, the causes of disappointing acquisition outcomes can only be reconciled by management. He argued that management can manage better the incremental variables through paying attention to all steps of an acquisition, therefore manipulating all related events with reference to each application to business and the demands of the acquisition. He identified a wide variety of control points, which affect the overall acquisition management process. He also developed ten decision factors as an interdependent aspect of an acquisition transaction. The ten decision factors include motivation, contact, information, sources, analysis, value, price, financing, contract, and implementation. Due to the logically progressive nature of the events within the mechanism of the transaction, he indicated that these ten decision factors were considered in the acquisition process. Most importantly, he stated that "Knowing what to do at the appointed time can make the difference between achieving success or failure".

Marks and Mirvis identified five key dimensions with which to focus top executives' attention and resources over the process of an acquisition. First, strategy can be described as managing the joining entity by consistently trying to align it to its strategic intents. Second, organization is described as establishing a new and healthier corporation. Third, people problems must be regarded as a crucial component and need considerable attention. Fourth, culture is described as building a desirable and healthy culture through the combination of the two firms. Finally, the transition management has an important role in developing a competent transition framework and plan. Marks and Mirvis further stated that the acquirer's core competence in a corporate acquisition, including planning, executing, and learning, will differentiate the future winners and the losers.

A Conceptual Framework of Acquisition Process

Constantly integrating the simultaneous incremental processes of strategy formulation and implementation is the heart of effective strategic management. It is important to acknowledge that the effective acquisition process must be synthesized and must simultaneously consider every factor affecting its outcome. Moreover, to maximize the acquiring firm's strategic gains, three general phases in the overall acquisition process, including the pre-acquisition management phase, the post-acquisition phase, and post-acquisition performance evaluation, must be planned as integral to one another, rather than as separate phases or a distinctive steps.

The post-acquisition outcome is the final product of an acquisition deal. In order to reach this outcome, there must be numerous specific processes involved. In a successful acquisition deal, each process has its own but crucial role. Therefore, successful acquisition management must view and execute each process seriously and in an integrated manner in order to achieve a desired final outcome, as well as enhance residual values. The acquisition process framework shown in Figure 1 represents the integrated and incremental approaches discussed so far. In sum, a systems approach can enhance the overall acquisition process. In order to capture the intended acquisition benefits, acquiring firms must perform their acquisition process in a deliberate manner that converts the acquisition intent to a realized one.

Mintzberg attacked the traditional planning approach because it inaccurately assumes that a firm's strategy is always the outcome of rational planning. Mintzberg argued that the core of strategy is that it relies on the role of process, rather than the plan. The key idea in Mintzberg's assertion is that strategies sometimes emerge from within a firm without any formal and predetermined plan. In other words, even if a firm did not possess any plan or intention, strategies can emerge from the lower levels of a firm. Indeed, sometimes a firm's appropriate strategies are a sudden response to unforeseen environments or circumstances. Most importantly, Mintzberg defined strategy as "a pattern in a stream of decisions and actions." The pattern represents a contingent product of either an intended or a planned strategy that is actually realized, or any unplanned or emergent strategies.

One of the acquirer's core competencies in corporate acquisition depends upon its capabilities to minimize emergent problems and maximize intended acquisition benefits, especially in the postacquisition management process. In other words, the acquirer must able to align its acquisition intent with post-acquisition integration, and must keep its strategic vision alive for a desired duration up to when necessary strategic changes are identified. An integrated/incremental framework of acquisition process acquisition process framework is shown in Figure 1, which can provide useful a conceptual framework for both practitioners and academics.

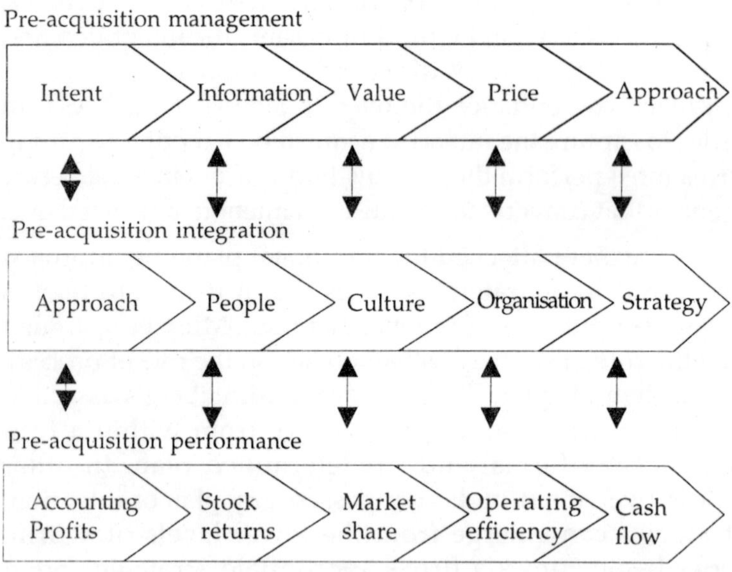

Figure 1: Integrated/incremental framework of acquisition process

This conceptual framework comprises fifteen dimensions (or constructs) in three phases of corporate acquisition: pre-acquisition management, post-acquisition integration, and post-acquisition performance. Further, each phase consists of five dimensions. The framework suggests that the acquirer must manage its acquisition intent throughout the overall acquisition process, which includes pre-acquisition management, post-acquisition integration, and post-acquisition performance evaluation, in an integrated/incremental manner to achieve the intended acquisition benefits. In addition, the framework suggests that the overall acquisition management process is more effective if acquirers adopt a process-driven approach rather than a sequential process. The incremental management of a series of important issues during the whole acquisition process must be executed based upon a pre-determined acquisition blue print. This is the most crucial factor in a successful acquisition bid.

Table 1 : Complementary concepts for a successful acquisition process

Concept	Content
Process Perspective in Corporate Acquisitions	The acquisition process is another factor in addition to strategic fit and organizational fit, that affects acquisition activities and outcomes
Rational Choice Perspective	Strategic fit between the acquirer and the target, and organizational fit in post-acquisition integration
Incremental Variables in Acquisition Management	Motivation-Contact-Information-Sources-Analyis-Value-Price- Financing-Contract-Implementation
Five Key Dimensions of an Acquisition Process	Strategy-Organization-People-Culture-Transition Management
Incrementalism in Strategy Formulation & Implementation	Constantly integrating the simultaneous incremental processes of strategy formulation and implementation is the heart of effective strategic management"
Intended vs. Emergent Strategy	The pattern represents a contingent product of either intended or planned strategy actually realized or any unplanned or emergent strategies.

The aspects of each dimension of integrated/incremental framework of acquisition process are discussed below in detail.

Pre-Acquisition Management Phase

If the acquirers can identify and prepare for a wide variety of factors in the pre-acquisition process, it can achieve not only smooth post-acquisition integration, but also can maximize post-acquisition performance.

Intent

There are number of reasons for a firm's strategic choice to grow through acquisition, rather than utilizing various internal growth strategies. Acquisition intent can be defined as a set of motives and/or objectives to undertake the purchase of a competitor or a business. There is a wide variety of causes and motives that have been identified in previous studies. Walter and Barney identified 20 managerial objectives of acquisitions. Here we reduced these 20 objectives to 5 broad dimensions.

- First, acquisitions are employed by acquirers to exploit both scale and scope economies.
- Second, managers utilize acquisition to control their external environmental interdependencies by securing input acquisition and output disposal.
- Third, acquisitions frequently are adopted to expand existing product/service lines and penetrate other markets.
- Fourth, acquirers undertake acquisition to enter a new line of businesses by reducing operating risks.
- Finally, acquisitions can be utilized to maximize financial capacity.

The motives of horizontal acquisition are operating efficiency gains through scale economies or market power. Dewey argued that acquisition is simply an efficient means of transition from a failing firm's inferior assets to successful or growing firms.

Information

The success of acquisition deals depends upon how the acquirer effectively evaluates value and potential synergies from acquiring the target. Gathering comprehensive and accurate, necessary information is critical to a successful deal. Information can be defined here as a wide variety of facts and data necessary to maintain and reinforce a purchasing decision.

In order to be successful in acquisitions, precise evaluations of target firms are the foremost task for acquirers. Salter and Weinhold argued that the acquirers frequently overestimate the value of the target, while underestimating the costs of realizing synergies. Markides and Willamson argued that acquisition relatedness must be measured as the degree of strategic assets.

In addition to collecting the target's information, identification of key success factors is important. Raab & Clark identified seven key success factors for a successful acquisition deal. They are:

- Recognize the magnitude and difficulty of the undertaking;
- Develop a realistic goal for the combined firm;
- Discover the right target;
- Seize top management cooperation without giving away the store;
- Plan the appropriate post-acquisition process early;
- Move rapidly; and
- Communication.

Value

The key goal of acquisition is to create value for the acquiring firm, and then maximize shareholders' wealth. The value of an acquisition usually depends upon a certain level of cash flow from the combined operating structures that leads to an increase in shareholders' wealth. Value can be defined as the worth of an acquisition deal created mainly from the anticipated synergistic benefits of the combining company. In horizontal acquisitions, acquisition value usually is created from anticipated synergistic benefits.

Sirower agrued that intended synergy will be realized when cash flow is increased, through either increased sales or reduced costs, or when the acquirer realizes the lowered discount rate that is incorporated in an acquirer's pre-acquisition stock price. Unlike Sirower, Chatterjee found that the value in acquisition is realized through restructuring the target by the acquiring firm, rather than through synergy itself.

Acquisition gains to service firms are not different than those that have been sought by manufacturing industry acquirers. McCann identified seven benefits of service firms' acquisitions as:

— increased market share,

— increased capacity to offer new products/services,

— improvements in brand & reputation,

— improved efficiency in resource allocations,

— increased scale economies,

— enlarged asset base, and

— acquisition of management expertise.

Grundy cautioned about the "iceberg of acquisition investment." Grundy found that some aspects of acquisition investment are highly observable, some are less observable, and other are murky or almost unobservable. Experienced acquirers can foresee the more visible aspects of acquisition deals better than inexperienced acquirers.

Price

The negotiation and determination of acquisition price has a tremendous impact on acquiring firms' post-acquisition performance. In general, purchase price is decided upon by the target's current competitive position within its industry. Unlike other investments, an acquisition investment usually should pay the premium over the target's current market value. Premiums have averaged between 40 and 50 percent in the first half of the 1990s.

Sirower found that the higher the acquisition premium paid, the higher the value lost. However, Smith and Hershman found that there is no clear correlation between purchasing price and acquisition premium and whether the deal creates value. Rappaport cautioned that to create value from acquisitions, the acquirers should consider that the present value of anticipated synergies must be greater than the premium paid.

Approach

Approach can be defined as the variety of surrounding procedures to persuade the target firm to accept and finalize an intended acquisition deal. There are several key factors which may determine value creation or value loss, including:

— the number of bidders;
— the bidder's acquisition approach (i.e., merger vs. tender offer);
— the method of payment (i.e., cash vs. stock);
— the type of acquisition (i.e., related vs. unrelated acquisition); and
— regulatory changes.

For example, in organizing an acquisition plan, the acquirer should determine which payment medium is appropriate to take over the target firm successfully. The acquiring company must choose the exchange medium among cash, debt, stock, or a combination of two methods. In terms of mode of acquisition, Jensen and Ruback found that the announcement period returns are higher for acquiring firms in tender offers than in mergers. According to Ikenberry, Lakonishok and Vermaelen, cash tender offers earn more than stock offers. Sirower and Loughran and Vijh found similar results, in that cash tender offers outperform stock mergers.

Post-Acquisition Integration Phase

The lack of systematic and thorough attention to potential problems of post-acquisition integration appears to reflect the difficulty of recognizing the process itself as part of the problem.

Approach

Approach is variety of surrounding procedures to reconcile a pre-determined acquisition intent to the target firm, while minimizing problems and obstacles. Napier identified three types of mergers. The first is an extension merger where the acquirer allows the target to maintain its independent position as usual, even after the deal is completed. The second is a collaborative merger, where both the acquirer and the target mix their operations, assets, and cultures to achieve anticipated synergistic benefits. The final is a redesign merger, where the acquiring firm makes significant changes in the target's overall operational and managerial practices.

In order to capture their intended acquisition benefits, acquiring firms should establish and execute an effective communication strategy to maintain a stable and comfortable work environment, especially for the target's employees. There are four primary dimensions of employee resistance when a firm announces change initiatives, including parochial self-interest, low tolerance for change, different assessments, and misunderstanding and lack of trust. To resolve these problems, Kotter and Schlesinger recommended extensive communications with employees. Raab and Clark also suggested that explicit communications with the target's employees must start immediately after the deal is announced.

People

People can be defined as a group of the merging company's organizational members, who have either positive or negative perceptions toward an acquisition deal. Previous studies identified the stress and negative impacts on a target's employees. One of them is that the loss of autonomy produced a negative effect on post-acquisition efforts, as well as on post-acquisition performance. Further, the acquiring firms should manage layoffs of target employees carefully, and they should consider other possible alternatives to replace layoff plans. Schweiger and DeNisi argued that a wide variety of communication problems and conflict between merging firms would reduce the effectiveness of postacquisition integration. The key source of a successful acquisition depends upon the effectiveness of the human side of the deal, such as employee-related issues.

There are two opinions about retaining the target's top executives. On the one hand, since the target's top executives are the valuable assets, their retention is one of the determinants of post-acquisition performance. On the other hand, the replacement of the target's top management team has facilitated the improvement of post-acquisition performance.

Culture

Cultural clash/distance can have a critical role in the post-acquisition integration process. In corporate acquisitions, some areas of the culture will be affected, including the maximization of employees' commitments to cooperate fully, to enhance sound integration during the radical changes brought about by an acquisition deal, and to establish a sense of unity throughout all the organizational members. Lack of cultural fit frequently is mentioned as a value-destructive factor in acquisitions. Cartwright and Cooper emphasized the importance of cultural fit by saying that that, "cultural fit and culture compatibility are well used but ill-defined expressions".

Culture can be defined as a set of important assumptions, such as norms, values and politics, that members of an organization share in common. Weber found a negative relationship between cultural distances and the effectiveness of post-acquisition integration. Moreover, Pablo identified that service firms tend to weigh cultural fit far more than manufacturing firms. In the post-acquisition integration stage, the alignment between management's philosophy and merging firms' culture has a critical impact on post-acquisition performance.

Organization

In order to improve resource allocation practices for combined firms, an effective and sound organizational structure is an essential in achieving acquisition benefits. Organizational design, reporting procedures, and various relationships in the work place must be established very quickly after the deal is completed. In order to create and sustain potential competitive advantages from acquisitions, an appropriate, new organizational design that leads to an effective resource allocation structure must be a necessary process.

Organization can be defined as a wide variety of organizational configurations, including formal and informal structures, systems, and processes.

In the related diversification strategy, to achieve potential benefits from acquisitions, merging firms need to establish proper internal mechanisms to efficiently transfer competencies and strategic assets across business units. When merging firms are well reorganized, they can achieve scale economies and can reduce redundancy in order to capture synergies. As more and more firms follow suit to utilize information technology, their dependence on information systems infrastructure has continually increased. One of the most important areas to which acquirers should pay particular attention is information systems and network infrastructure. The ignorance of information systems, both in pre- and post-acquisition processes, will have negative impacts on the immediate execution of a wide variety of operations for merging firms.

Strategy

Strategy can be defined as a set of consistent alignment efforts to achieve the long-term goals of the merging company based upon the acquisition intent. It is crucial to renew or reinvent the target firm and/or combined firm's overall strategy to rèalize acquisition objectives. Further, it is essential to match acquisition vision and management processes and systems. Sirower also emphasized the importance of the alignment between the strategic vision of the acquisition deal and the operating strategy.

The perating strategy must be executed immediately after the deal is closed, and it must be developed based upon a new set of competition analyses. After the deal is completed, the operating strategy must address clearly how the combined firm is to seize a competitive position that is incorporated within the entire value chain of the business. The combined firm must be able to improve its competitive methods and/or to extend other competitive methods to compete effectively in order to achieve its intended synergistic benefits and sustain its competitive advantages.

Post-Acquisition Performance Evaluation

It is important to evaluate the postacquisition performance of the combined firm based upon pre-determined, definite evaluation criteria. In general, financial measures are utilized to evaluate post-acquisition performance. Cochran and Wood identified that there is no consensus on an appropriate measure of financial performance. Given the ambiguities and difficulties in assessing accurately the impact of acquisitions on performance, it becomes crucial to develop proper key performance gauges of post-acquisition performance.

Accounting Profits

Accounting profitability (i.e., return on sales, return on equity, return on net assets) is one of the typical measures used as an indicator of postacquisition performance. Grant, Jammine and Thomas argued that accounting profits more effectively measure the direct results of post-acquisition performance than stock price, which reflects the future expectations of investors.

Stock returns

There are two measures of post-acquisition performance in terms of stock price. Most prior studies adopted the stock price changes surrounding acquisition announcement dates as a performance indicator. On the other hand, relatively few studies have investigated the long-run performance of acquiring firms after acquisitions. Stock returns is the acquirer's stock price changes either surrounding the acquisition announcement date or certain periods of time after the deal is announced.

Operations cash flow

Since stock performance studies cannot identify the real economic value gains from acquisitions, post-acquisition operating cash flow is a better indicator to measure post-acquisition performance. Operations cash flow is sales, minus cost of goods sold and selling administrative expenses, plus depreciation and goodwill expenses.

Market share

Some previous studies have utilized changes in market share as measures of competitive performance. Brush argued that, "Market share and change in market share are the only measures of business performance available at the level of disaggregation necessary for intraindustry analysis at the business level of the firm for all manufacturing companies". Market share is the ratio of sales revenue of the combined firm to the total sales revenue of all firms in the particular industry, including the merged firm itself.

Operating efficiency

Post-acquisition operating efficiency is the key for achieving the anticipated acquisition benefits for a combining firm. Brush argued that operational synergy is a key acquisition objective and a determinant of post-acquisition performance. Linn and Switzer found that acquirers experienced significantly worse industry- and size-adjusted operating performance for up to five years following an acquisition transaction. In the hotel industry, occupancy rate, RevPAR (Revenue Per Available Room), and ADR (Average Daily Room Rate) are the most fundamental indicators in measuring operating efficiencies.

8

Investment Guidelines

Investing in hotels and motels is considered by many to be a high-risk use of time and capital. The investor not only acquires an interest in a volatile form of real property but also participates in the highly specialized business of operating a service-oriented going concern. Where the lodging facility includes food, beverage, banquet, and recreational facilities, the risk and accompanying aggravation are often multiplied tenfold. Yet, despite the sometimes dire consequences associated with such investments, investors continue to be drawn to the status and glamour of hotels as well to the potential for gain. An investment in the lodging industry, whether it be for the purpose of acquiring an existing facility or developing a completely new one, requires a certain amount of research regarding both the industry as a whole and the investment itself.

The evolution of the lodging industry is, of course, closely related to the economic history of the world. Usually, the health of the industry can be gauged by the condition of the economy as a whole. Prosperous times for the nations typically mean increased room and occupancy rates and the construction of more lodging facilities. When the economy falters, leisure and business travelers tend to stay home or spend less on accommodations when travel is necessary. Internal industry cycles also have a strong effect on the lodging industry. The most important of these is the continually changing relationship between room demand and room supply. For example, hotel construction is fueled by several factors other than simple demand. The availability of funds is often a determining factor. Oversupply, often the result of periods of increased construction activity, has meant stagnation for the industry, even when the economy as a whole performs well.

Along with the evolution of lodging products and the identification and pursuit of specific segments of the lodging market, the ownership and management of lodging facilities have undergone many changes. The industry, which began with entrepreneurs who owned and managed individual properties, has come to be dominated by national and international chains. At one time, the chains built and owned the properties on which their names were displayed, but the trend in the industry is for many of the major hotel chains to develop and manage properties for outside investors. This fundamental change has dramatically increased the number of individuals and corporate entities involved in hotel projects.

In addition to a familiarity with the basic elements of the lodging industry and the economic trends that affect it, an understanding of the nature of the national supply of lodging and the national demand for lodging is essential in order to correctly make the crucial decisions affecting an investment, such as the choice of a particular market or product.

Whether a hotel investment entails the development of a new property or the acquisition of an existing facility, proper planning is necessary for success. The following lists outline the steps that must be taken to acquire or develop a lodging facility. Some of the steps are appropriate for both the development and acquisition process, while others are unique to only one. The order of the various steps is not fixed and some may be performed concurrently.

Hotel Acquisition:

- *Planning stage:*
  - Select a region of the United States.
  - Narrow the selection to several cities or market areas.
  - Look for a market niche.
  - Look for a product (i.e., available properties).
  - Perform a preliminary economic market study and appraisal.
  - Implementation stage:
  - Tie up the property with a letter of intent, option, or contract.
  - Negotiate the terms of the sale.
  - Go to contract on the property.
  - Line up an operator.
  - Line up a franchise.
  - Commission a formal economic market study and appraisal.
  - Line up mortgage financing.
  - Line up equity financing.

Hotel Development:

- *Planning stage:*
  - Select a region of the United States.
  - Narrow the selection to several cities or market areas.
  - Look for a market niche.
  - Look for a product (i.e., available sites).
  - Perform a preliminary economic market study and appraisal.

— Implementation stage:
— Tie up the property with a letter of intent, option, or contract.
— Obtain zoning and permits.
— Assemble the project team.
— Line up an operator and franchise.
— Prepare architectural plans and estimate project costs.
— Commission a formal economic market study and appraisal.
— Line up a mortgage.
— Line up equity capital.

Selecting Lodging Market

The first step in both hotel acquisition and development planning is to determine where to begin the search for suitable hotels to acquire or sites to develop. The investors should evaluate various regions, using data and analytical techniques to determine whether they should be considered further or rejected. Some of the important factors that investors should consider are the following:

— *Proximity to home office.* Hotels are labor-intensive businesses that require constant supervision and direction. When acquiring or developing a lodging facility, investors are well-advised to keep it close to home so that it can be given their full attention. Supervising lodging operations scattered over a wide geographic area is of course possible, but to do so requires a level of expertise that can be gained only through significant industry experience.

— *Signs of economic growth.* Regions of the country exhibiting strong growth trends are generally better suited for hotel investing than are regions that are economically stagnant.

— *Competitive environment.* The hotel investor should carefully evaluate the regional supply of competitive lodging facilities in conjunction with his study of economic growth. Even if economic trends are favorable, an adverse competitive environment brought about by the oversupply of hotel rooms can make a region an undesirable location for acquiring or developing a lodging facility.

Once the investor has selected a particular region, he should use similar criteria to choose specific market areas in which to focus his investigations. The demand for transient accommodations and the competitive supply are once again the key factors to be considered when analyzing potential market areas.

After the market area has been determined, the next step is to find a market niche, which is a unique market position or a particular market for which a product may be suited. When evaluating a market area, the hotel investor first looks for situations that exhibit a need for a specific hotel product. At the same time, consideration is also given to protective characteristics known as barriers to entry, which might include restrictive zoning or license approval processes, limited suitable land or acquisition opportunities, rapidly escalating construction costs, and the unavailability of an appropriate chain affiliation or management company. A unique market position may quickly change to an overbuilt position if no barriers to entry exist and other competitive products can enter the market without much difficulty.

Finding the appropriate market niche not only is an important consideration for a proposed hotel development but can be equally critical when it becomes necessary to reposition an existing property. A hotel can be repositioned through a renovation or upgrading, change of franchise affiliation, or the introduction of new management.

Property and Site Selection

Once the type of hotel has been determined on the basis of the evaluation of market niches, the investor must start to look for available hotels if an existing property is desired, or suitable sites if a new development is desired.

Real estate brokers are the best source of information regarding the availability of property for sale. When looking for an existing hotel, investors often use the services of a broker whose practice is concentrated in the lodging industry. A knowledgeable hotel broker can save considerable time and effort by showing only properties that meet the investor's particular criteria. When looking for potential hotel sites, it is best to use a land broker familiar with the local area-particularly the zoning regulations, building codes, and related laws. One of the most difficult aspects of accomplishing a hotel development is obtaining the necessary zoning changes and variances.

A knowledgeable land broker understands these issues and can direct the developer to suitable sites requiring minimal zoning changes and approvals. Brokers are compensated by the seller with commissions based on a percentage of the sales price-generally 1 percent to 4 percent for existing hotels and 4 percent to 10 percent for vacant land.

Real estate brokers are agents for the seller; as such, they work for, are loyal to, and are paid by the property owner. Sometimes buyers of existing hotels or developable sites find it advantageous to employ either a broker or a property search firm to research potential investment opportunities. This alternative is sometimes effective, because a search firm is often able to obtain leads on hotels for sale before they actually go on the market. The same hotel knowledge and experience is necessary for a hotel search firm as a hotel broker. The fee arrangement for a hotel search depends largely on the area covered; sometimes fees are based on an hourly or per diem rate, a flat fee, or some formula related to the number of hotels actually acquired by the client. Buyers can also research the market and successfully locate potential products on their own, but usually only if the buyer is familiar with the local area and knows all the property owners and potential sellers or if the buyer is a major, well-known buyer of lodging facilities and is likely to receive solicitations directly from potential sellers. By dealing directly with the seller, the buyer can avoid paying a fee to a broker or a search firm, and thus eliminate a considerable expense, which is ultimately reflected in the purchase price of the property.

Market Study and Appraisal

Before any money is committed to the purchase of the property, prudent investors perform or commission a thorough preliminary economic market study and appraisal. The information yielded by this analysis is used to determine the type of hotel and facilities best suited to the location and the type of management and franchise affiliation (if any) that would be the most effective.

Another important product of a market study is a forecast of the revenues and expenses that the subject property can be expected to realize. This information is vital to the buyer during the negotiation of the sale of the property, because it can be used to determine the value of the facility.

The first step in evaluating a proposed investment is to analyze the site of the proposed or existing property. The suitability of the site for hotel operations is one of the most important determinants of the success of an investment. The site analysis involves such factors as the physical suitability of the land, access and visibility, the availability of utilities and other services, and the applicable zoning regulations.

Once a particular site has been selected, the area in which it is located must be evaluated. Generally, this evaluation includes both the immediate neighborhood of the site and its market area. The extent of the relevant neighborhood can usually be determined by simple observation of the surrounding area, including roads and land-use patterns. The market area, on the other hand, is often harder to identify because it involves a larger area and depends on more abstract factors (e.g., competition and travel patterns).

An important step in any hotel investment is an examination of the supply of lodging facilities in the subject area. Before the success of the proposed hotel investment can be determined, the appraiser must first determine the degree to which other hotels in the area would compete with the subject property.

After the supply of hotels has been evaluated, the existing demand must be quantified to determine its ability to support a new hotel or the acquisition of an existing facility. The demand analysis can be performed using one of two methods: the demand generator build-up approach or the lodging activity build-up approach.

In conjunction with the analyses of local supply and demand, the appraiser must determine the competitive positions of all the local facilities and how the subject property would fit into this picture. Generally, this task involves determining the current market share, average room rate, and occupancy rate of the existing competition. Once this determination has been made, the appraiser can forecast these variables for the subject property.

One of the final steps in the preliminary appraisal is to forecast the income and expenses of the proposed hotel investment. The income projection focuses on a hotel's main categories of revenue, such as rooms, food and beverage, and telephone income. The expense projection examines a hotel's main items of expense, such as rooms, food and beverage, telephone, administrative, management, and marketing costs.

A property valuation, along with the forecasts of revenue and expense, allows the appraiser to make a recommendation regarding the feasibility of a proposed hotel investment. The first step in a property valuation is to determine the overall worth of the subject property. This step entails appraising an existing hotel or forecasting the value of a proposed property. This value is contrasted against the cost of the property, which is either the cost of acquisition or of construction. The three basic methods for performing a property valuation are : the cost approach, the sales comparison approach, and the income capitalization approach.

Ownership

The form of hotel ownership is a very important decision that is usually based on tax, legal, or business considerations. For example, an owner might choose to form a corporation instead of individual ownership in order to limit his personal liability.

The following kinds of ownerships are possiblie in hotel industry

1. Individual ownership
2. Concurrent ownership
3. Partnership
4. Regular corporation
6. Limited liability company
7. Trust
8. Real estate investment trust

Financing

Financial and debt sources of hotel industry can be grouped into the following two categories:

1. Institutions that originate mortgages and maintain portfolios of both mortgages and real estate equities, including:
   - Commercial banks;
   - Life insurance companies;
   - Private credit companies; and
   - Pension funds.
2. Investment conduits, which are primarily entities that invest in hotel real estate mortgages and pass through income and gain to investors (both private individuals and institutions), including:
   - Real estate limited partnerships (RELPs);
   - Real estate investment trusts (REITs); and
   - Commercial mortgage-backed securities (CMBS).
3. Mortgage financing, which is how most hotels are financed. Topics covered include:
   - Types of Mortgage loans; and
   - Obtaining a hotel mortgage.

Exchange of Hotels

The major issues related to the buying and selling of hotel properties are

- The first is the importance of hiring a professional broker when selling a hotel property.
- The second is the like-kind exchange.

An exchange of hotels, or an exchange of business property for a desired hotel property, is a creative means of acquiring a new property. This method can offer unique planning opportunities for the hospitality or business owner who wishes to relocate to another market. It can also provide significant tax savings for a new owner, because appreciated property can be exchanged without incurring any tax on the appreciated gain.

Franchise Affiliation

Two of the most important steps in the hotel investment process are obtaining a franchise affiliation and selecting a hotel management company. The choice of a franchise affiliation is an important decision in a hotel investment that should be made as early in the acquisition or development process as possible. Even more so than a management company, a franchise company will want the opportunity to participate in decisions regarding designs and specifications for a lodging facility, because most have companywide standards that must be met by each of their properties. An early decision also enables the property owner to accurately determine the cost of the franchise affiliation and use the information when analyzing the economics of the project.

Property Management

Whether the project in question is a development or an acquisition, a management company should be retained as early as possible in the process. In the case of a development, a management company should be brought in before any significant amount of time is spent on architectural drawings, so that the management company will have the opportunity to provide suggestions regarding the layout and general design of the facility. Securing a management company early on is even more important for a hotel acquisition, because the company will often be able to generate valuable information regarding the projected operating performance of the property, which can be a critical factor for the purchaser during the negotiation of the sale of the property. In addition, the management company will indicate what changes must be made to the property if improvements are required in order to meet the company's operating standards. This input will also have an effect on the negotiating position of the buyer.

The two basic types of management companies are: first-tier operators and second-tier operators. It examines all of the important considerations in choosing a management company and looks at the actual contract negotiation process. It also compares the hiring of individual managers to the hiring of a management company.

Management Contracts

The proper execution of the management contract is a vital step for the successful development of the hotel investment. Each party must be able to negotiate the contract with a full understanding of the consequences of including or disallowing a particular provision. If either party is permitted to include provisions that are disproportionately favorable to its position, the working relationship between the parties can be severely damaged.

9

Forces for Change

The traditional transactional work of Human Resource (HR) is rapidly becoming a commodity; at many companies, there are signifi- cant cost savings to be realized by treating it in this manner. Top managers are increasingly aware of the efficiencies that new technologies can provide, and they are putting pressure on the HR function to reduce costs as never before. There is a growing demand for expertise regarding the deployment and management of human capital and organizational capability; the HR function can and should provide that expertise. Managers at all levels increasingly need strategic guidance about how they deploy their workforce and build their organizations in order to fulfill company goals.

In order to respond effectively to both pressures, the HR function must simultaneously create transaction efficiencies and transformational changes. But substantive change in the nature of a staff function's work and role is rare. What's more, when such change does occur, it is usually driven by forces outside the department, such as a merger, a divestiture, a technology change, a change in the economy, or a new business strategy.

Rarely do staff functions step up to reinvent themselves. Currently, most HR leaders can still choose whether they will respond to change or whether they will lead change. HR executives still have the opportunity to shape how they and the HR function respond to the demands that their function is experiencing. To us, the path is clear. We believe that HR executives who stick with the status quo and maintain a focus on transactional work will soon become obsolete.

Changing Supply and Demand

To assess the nature and extent of the change required of HR, imagine a simple demand-supply model for businesses and apply that model to the future of HR. Start by stepping back and considering the major factors that are placing new or shifting demands on businesses today. Since top managers grapple with these issues, HR professionals need to understand and respond to them in order to add value and establish their worth:

Customer-firm Interactions

Customers have more access to information and are more informed than ever before. As a result, customer expectations are higher than ever before, and competition for customer share is greater than ever before. Customers expect—and usually get—lower cost and higher-quality goods and services; as a result, they put pressure on organizations to reduce their own costs even as they strive to improve quality. HR directly affects operating costs because of the cost of its own operation and because it is partially responsible for a major expense: wages and benefits. In addition, the quality of HR services influences product and service costs and quality because the quality of HR services affects employee behavior and performance.

Increasing Targeting Key Customers

At eBay, 10 percent of the customers purchase 90 percent of the products; in the airline industry, 10 percent of the customers provide 40 percent of revenue and 60 percent of profit. Financial service firms strive for share of wallet; food product firms seek share of stomach. In each of these cases, new customer realities have established new rules for winning; customer share is now more important in these scenarios than market share. To gain a critical customer share, companies must build a value proposition uniquely tailored to a particular target customer. Amazon, for example, knows the book buying patterns of those who buy more books and can tailor its offerings to those target customers.

One way to increase customer intimacy in key customer groups is to involve these customers in significant company activities that are designed to improve service levels. By involving customers in HR activities, HR practices may be used to create intimacy with targeted customers. When leaders worry about employees as if they are customers and customers as if they are employees, both customers and employees are more engaged and committed. When HR practices are used to align both employees and customers, both employee and customer share grows.

Evolving Information Technology

Information is increasingly ubiquitous and also increasingly easier to access and manipulate. This trend has significant implications for business-to-business, business-to-supplier, and business-to-employee relationships. It is also the foundation of e-business operations. Information technology allows for warehousing the kinds of customer data that enable companies to identify specific customers and determine their buying criteria. Such data also allow customers to be targeted for life, as companies continually update their knowledge of customers' behaviors and buying criteria.

Information about employees allows companies to personalize employee rewards and better understand their employees' expertise, potential to contribute value, and likely career paths. Information warehouses can make it possible for organizations to analyze employee data to determine the costs and effectiveness of their HR practices and the degree to which they support key business strategies. Information, in other words, increasingly is both a revenue source and a source of competitive advantage. Computer access companies like Time Warner and Yahoo increasingly make money on the information they track on their users.

Firms with better information about customers, for example, can make decisions to move into new markets more quickly than their competition. Unilever tracks consumer buying patterns based on a number of demographic inputs such as household income, marital status, size of household, and household gender makeup. Using this information, Unilever targets its marketing not only to a region or geography, but also to a particular household through coupons and advertising. Consumer information becomes a source of competitive advantage because Unilever knows better than its competitors what consumers want and expect.

Similarly, firms with enhanced understanding of their employees' strengths and weaknesses are better able to make strategic decisions that will stick and succeed. A company that understands at the outset whether it has the capabilities to expand into a new market and where it needs to bolster its capabilities has a competitive advantage over companies that do not know themselves as well.

The implications of the growing importance of information for HR are obvious: HR must continue updating its systems and provide current and accurate data on employees, HR practices, and organizational outcomes. HR must also help turn information into informed choices so that data are not just warehoused but used to improve decision making. HR must help business leaders generate and use information to help their organizations compete. HR systems must support change, using technology faster and deploying it more routinely. HR practices also need to adjust to the increasing availability of information technology.

Staffing with information technology (such as computer databases and Internet screening of candidates) allows employers to identify and screen a broader array of candidates. Development with information technology (IT) allows for remote learning. Compensation management with technology allows for decisions to be made rapidly and accurately. IT-based selfservice, when it comes to HR administration, can reduce the cost of HR as well as provide faster service.

Changing Shape of Hospitality Industry

Mergers and acquisitions continue to occur, and in some significant cases, they have crossed traditional industry boundaries to create convergence across boundaries. For example, the merger and alliance activity in the airline industry has redefined the industry. Today, convergence means that airlines sometimes compete with organizations outside their industry. For example, frequent flier programs are key assets to the airlines, but now these companies play in the same competitive arena as retail stores, telephone companies, and restaurants in deploying frequent flier benefits.

Similarly, financial service firms worry about customers banking through Internet firms, about supermarkets performing financial services, and about traditional manufacturing firms like General Motors and General Electric performing financing functions. Industry consolidation also means that products that were once in the purview of only one industry now cross boundaries. Computer monitors may become televisions and vice versa; telephones are now cameras.

Vehicle on-line services like General Motors's On-Star make the automotive company a player in communication services; utility firms now offer control services to manage home and commercial temperature; and the electronics inside appliances now allow washing machines, refrigerators, and the like to be directly connected to central services for maintenance and monitoring usage. As industries evolve in this manner, leaders seek creative and alternative ways to leverage their organizations' core competencies and organizational capabilities across industry boundaries. At the heart of both are people. HR systems that help people conceive innovative ways to define and navigate industry boundaries can become an important competitive edge.

Changing Investors' Assessments Value

Recent research on market value has shown that the tangible financial assets of a firm predict less of its total market value today than in the past. A firm's total market value thus increasingly comes from the intangible assets that a firm possesses. In exploring intangibles, investors look behind the financial numbers to determine the market value of a firm. They examine intangibles that predict future results, and this affects the current market value of corporations. Intangibles such as quality of leadership, speed of response, ability to innovate, capacity to integrate acquisitions, accountability for results, culture, and talent are becoming a central part of a firm's total shareholder value proposition.

Leaders have the primary responsibility for creating sustainable intangible value, but HR professionals can help in shaping intangibles. The goal is to build organizations whose long-term viability is ensured by the way the organization operates internally. HR professionals can contribute by developing HR systems that are designed to attract, deploy, motivate, and engage human capital in ways that create superior intangibles.

Consider that the ethics and values of senior management are among the most critical intangibles. When senior leaders are seen as greedy and excessively self-interested, investors discount the market value of the firm's financial performance. When leaders are forthcoming with problems and honest in assessments—that is, when they operate ethically—investors award firms positive intangible value. Ethics and integrity have become a social agenda that leaders must explicitly acknowledge and manage. This agenda has a number of dimensions. For example, it encompasses legal issues. When leaders violate the laws that govern organizations and society, either explicitly through their actions or implicitly by turning away from and ignoring others' behavior, they fall into an ethics black hole that results in lost credibility. Customers, investors, and employees lose faith.

Leaders who assume large and visible organizational roles must live to a high standard, their behavior beyond reproach. Even the appearance of misdoing often leads to an erosion of confidence from critical stakeholders. Leaders, because of their status, economic rewards, and opportunities to influence, must be cautious about their behavior and the ways in which others view that behavior.

One important way that organizations shape social values is through their HR practices. For example, rewards often communicate a social value. When the only performance metric is financial returns pay for performance becomes a way of signaling what the organization values. If performance includes a more balanced scorecard, then leaders will change their behavior to reflect what is measured. Leaders need confidants who advise them on social issues and offer candid counsel and feedback on their behavior and on how to make informed social choices. HR professionals can be a voice for creating a social agenda and a source of candid feedback on ethical issues.

Social Trends

Many social trends affect how leaders and organizations act. The recent heightened emphasis on exemplary leadership behavior is one. The widening gap between the haves and have-nots is another. This bifurcation of the population has become more acute with the development of technology. The haves have access to computers and the Web, which leverages their knowledge and breadth of influence. The have-nots have little access to technology, which limits their scope of influence and thinking.

Business leaders often experience primarily the haves in their dayto- day work and may not be sensitive to the have-nots. Sometimes leaders live in "affluence ghettos," whereby they work with people who are educated, successful, and ambitious; they live in the same neighborhoods as these people; their children attend the same schools; they socialize in the same areas; and they shop in the same stores.

An affluence ghetto constrains a leader's perception of the range of people who might work for or buy from his or her organization and in doing so limits the organization's potential to grow. Leaders need to be sensitive to the reality that their background is not always the background of those who buy the company's products or of employees who make and sell those products. For the benefit of their organizations, they need to seek talented employees from multiple sources and leverage diverse backgrounds into common approaches.

Impact of Globalization

The realities of globalization, with information, ideas, jobs, and people moving readily around the world, create complex leadership challenges. It is well known that leaders must learn to create global organizations that can both leverage global scale and adapt locally, move information quickly from one site to another, manage the diversity of cultures while maintaining unity of focus, and manage employees in dispersed operations around the globe. It is much less understood that HR issues are often central to global success. Yet knowing how to attract, motivate, and retain talent in one region of the world does not necessarily mean knowing how to do the same in another region. Reward systems may also vary. Being global in business requires being global in organizational design, people, and HR practices.

Winning also requires creating an organization that accomplishes stated goals. Organization is more than structure; it is the set of capabilities a firm possesses. Capabilities represent what the firm is able to do well, its culture, and its unique identity. These capabilities derive from an integrated set of HR investments, where HR practices of staffing, training, rewards, communication, organizational design, workplace design, and so forth are aligned around building capability.

The reality of the competitive business environment is that organizations can be successful only when they focus on doing those activities that help accomplish strategic objectives through core competencies and organizational capabilities. If organizations lack all the core competencies and organizational capabilities they need to succeed, they must build relationships with partners who can fill the gaps. The implications of this point are profound: filling gaps in vital capabilities can lead organizations to outsource any number of functions, from manufacturing to staff services such as IT and HR management. The key is ensuring that each partner supplies clear value so that the whole, which can be seen in the value delivered to customers, reduced costs, and ensuing profits, is greater than the sum of its parts.

Organizational forms are changing. The traditional hierarchy governed by rules, roles, and responsibilities is often not the best way to manage. Instead of rules that govern how employees behave, more and more employees do what they do because of unity of interests. Management by mind-set, or common goals or values, often needs to replace management by objectives. Employees need to focus on getting the work done regardless of formal roles, and managers need to encourage and facilitate such independent and responsible behavior. Because of these changes, new organizational forms need to be used. Leaders need to allocate critical tasks to individuals rather than relying on an organizational chart.

Instead of responsibilities laid out in job descriptions and profiles, employees need to join and work in task forces to define and deliver work. Because of the importance of organization as a source of competitive advantage, companies need expertise in organizational effectiveness. They need to develop new designs and determine how to develop the competencies and capabilities they require in order to implement their strategies. HR can play an important role both in developing strategies that are based on competencies and capabilities and helping organizations and their leaders develop the right competencies and capabilities. Success in today's business environment requires leaders who are not only aware of but also sensitive to the many changes and demands that organizations face. Managers need to learn to influence less through formal position and more through relationships.

If leaders fail to respond to these increasing demands, they will be replaced by executives who do. The well-chronicled, increasing rate of CEO failure often can be traced to their inability to respond to one or more of the new demands.Sometimes failed CEOs were unable to anticipate technology or customer change, sometimes their actions violated social and legal norms, and sometimes they failed to engage their employees in the process of change.The need for effective managers and leaders at all levels is being felt by virtually every organization. HR is clearly well positioned to help organizations meet this need, and its future undoubtedly will be significantly influenced by how effectively it helps organizations meet it.

Opportunities of HR Professionals

HR professionals have to create value for employees, customers, investors, and their organization.

Value for Employees: Many employees want opportunities to learn and to grow. HR professionals need to build a new employee value proposition that both increases and clarifies what employees should give to their organization and what organizations should give to their employees. The new business realities require employees who are able to contribute more productivity, knowledge, and skill than ever before. And when employees make these contributions, they must get more back from the firm. As employee demographics shift, what employees get back may be more focused on accomplishment and development.

Employees may get opportunities to learn and grow, a chance to work for an organization with a significant purpose or meaning, a team of peers who share values and offer a cohesive community, access to information about where the organization is headed and why, and flexible policies and practices that adapt to each employee's personal life.

HR professionals can play a major role in crafting HR practices and employee policies that simultaneously articulate what employees are expected to contribute and to receive. HR practices should also be customized to support the business strategy of the organization. Finally,

HR can help make a workplace more employee-friendly by offering high-quality user-friendly administrative services.

Value for Customers: In the new business realities, customer share often becomes the dominant criterion. Customer share represents the percentage of total volume a customer does that is garnered by one firm over the lifetime of the customer. Customer share requires that leaders identity target customers—those customers who have both scale (because of their volume of purchases) and opportunity (because of their potential for growth). Once leaders identify target customers, they are able to work to gain share of those customers. Gaining customer share with targeted customers comes when leaders know how to build more intimate connections with customers.

Some connection may come from involving customers in strategic and product decisions by using focus groups, market research, or strategic planning. It may come by using technology to directly link to customers. eBay tracks the buying patterns of its frequent customers (time of day, time of month, type of good purchased, and other parameters) to target key customers. Customer connection may also come from including customers in HR practices of staffing, training, compensation, and organizational design. Target customers can participate in staffing by recommending or screening candidates, in training by delivering or attending the training activity, in compensation by evaluating performance, and in organizational design by participating in task forces.

HR contributes to customer share when HR practices are explicitly linked to meeting the requirements of target customers and when target customers actually participate in defining those HR practices. For example, one hotel chain uses a group of customers in defining the competencies required of its hotel management. These frequent guests of the hotel could articulate what they as target customers wanted to experience in their travels. By working with these customers, the HR practices for hiring, training, and rewarding were defined according to customer requirements. This hotel chain, in fact, often includes customer input when implementing HR practices.

Customers are among those who interview candidates for key positions. They present a portion of an orientation or training seminar. They offer data about their experiences that become part of the appraisal process. The goal of these activities is that the hotel chain will have actions aligned with target customer expectations so that target customers will consistently select this hotel. To meet the customer share demand and focus HR practices on customers, HR professionals must look beyond HR administration and become much more customer sensitive. They need to know who the target customers are, why they chose one vendor over another, and how existing HR practices can be tweaked to serve customers better.

Value for Investors: Investors increasingly are looking beyond and behind the financial numbers to intangibles, which may range from more visible issues such as brand and research and development investment to organizational capability issues such as quality of leadership. With intangible assets, leaders may create a "story line" for investors that increases credibility and confidence. As a result of this confidence, market value goes up. For example, Herman Miller has more than double the market capitalization than Steelcase, a firm about twice its size, because Herman Miller has known organizational capabilities that give it a higher intangible value in the eyes of investors.

Intangible value comes when investors know about and have confidence that the infrastructure of the firm is able to ensure future earnings. Many of the intangibles investors value come from HR practices. When a firm has a reputation for better talent, faster time to market, more innovative products and services, better collaboration, more ability to learn and share information, and accountability for results, investors value the firm more highly. HR professionals face the demand of performing so that their work adds to the intangible value of their organization.

In order for HR professionals to meet investor demands, they must become knowledgeable about who the firm's investors are, what investor expectations are, and how to communicate to investors the intangibles that matter most. HR professionals may also provide intellectual leadership in performing intangible audits where the intangibles are identified and evaluated and plans made for improvement. HR costs are part of the total expenses of doing business. Controlling and getting a good return on investments in training and other HR programs can contribute to the bottom line of a corporation.

Value for Organizations: Some leaders have taken a balanced scorecard approach to measuring organizational effectiveness by focusing on employees, customers, and investors. They believe they can "succeed" by focusing on these three stakeholders. However, we do not think so. The organization is a critical, separate, and independent stakeholder. It has a culture or personality that endures beyond any single leader and any single program. Organizations have enduring patterns that take on a life of their own. These patterns cause some employees to join and others to leave. These patterns become expectations of old customers and attract new customers. They give investors confidence when they support a credible business strategy.

These patterns or culture become the capabilities embedded within an organization. Most successful organizations have something they are known for that defines them; for example, Southwest Airlines is known for service and Disney theme parks for family entertainment. Firm identity should come from HR policies and practices. It needs to be developed based on a business strategy that recognizes the importance of shared culture. A firm's identity should focus HR work on deliverables more than

10

Tourism in Europe

Many factors affect the demand for tourism, including increases in time for leisure activities and their social importance, economic growth, and changes in demographic factors, behaviour and expectations. The choice of destination remains determined mainly by scenery and climate.

The tourism industry recognises the need to maintain its main assets, for example the attractiveness of destinations. While it is now generally recognised that tourism will be a successful industry only if it is managed in an ecological and sustainable manner, some efforts are still needed to move towards a broader and more integrated approach. At the international level, the United Nations Commission on Sustainable Development (UNCSD) and the Convention on Biological Diversity (CBD) have targeted tourism as a priority policy area. At the regional level, the Mediterranean countries, the Alpine countries and the Baltic countries have initiated actions to promote sustainable tourism.

The European Union (EU) Council adopted a resolution in May 2002 on the need to improve the coordination of policies that affect tourism. An Agenda 21 programme includes an integrated evaluation of tourism activity throughout the EU, the development of an integration strategy for the sector and the elaboration of harmonised indicators of sustainable development for tourism.

Important Tourism Patterns

Tourism is an important industry in Europe. Europe offers the greatest diversity and density of attractions - coastal zones, islands, mountains, historical sites and countryside. The region has long been the world's favourite tourist destination, with almost 60 % of the world market share. International arrivals are expected to grow by 50 % to around 720 million per year by 2020, with a doubling of air traffic in Europe. In the EU, the sector represents 30 % of total external trade in services, 6 % of employment and contributes 7 % of GDP (12 % if indirect effects are included).

During the past two decades, international tourism in Europe increased by an average of 3.8 % per year. The World Tourism Organisation (WTO, 2001b) forecasts an annual increase of 3.1 % over the period 1995-2020, which is one percentage point more than the anticipated economic growth. The three most visited countries in the world, France, Spain and Italy, already accounted for 24 % of the world's total arrivals in 1999 and will remain in this position even if their total share is expected to fall. At the same time, some other regions are becoming more attractive as a result of economic transition and the opening of borders, with a huge potential for tourism development.

The countries of eastern Europe, the Caucasus and central Asia (EECCA), recorded the biggest growth over the period 1995-99, with tourist arrivals approximately doubling. The biggest growth (4.8 % per year up to 2020) is expected in central and eastern Europe (CEE). Poland, the Czech Republic, Hungary and Turkey accounted for 81 % of CEE arrivals in 1999. However, most tourist trips are not international, but within the country of origin. In 1995, WTO estimated that total domestic tourist arrivals numbered about 5.6 billion worldwide, with 567 million tourists travelling outside their own country (699 million in 2000). In Europe, domestic tourism accounts for 20-90 % of all tourist trips, from less than 20 % in Luxemburg, Croatia and the Czech Republic to around 90 % in Germany, Finland and Romania.

European tourists chose the sea (63 %), mountains (25 %), cities (25 %) and the countryside (23 %) as holiday destinations in 1997 (European Commission, 1998). However, tourists are becoming more interested in higher quality tourism experiences, particularly in natural and cultural sites; nature, beauty and calm are the first criteria for choosing a destination, before price. During recent years, the length of vacations has increased, which gives more time for tourism and leisure. Europeans now take multiple holidays rather than extending the length of their main holiday.

In the Netherlands for instance, the average number of vacations per person increased from 1.21 to 1.71 between 1966 and 1997, and the number of short breaks doubled in comparison to long vacations. UK residents who travelled within their own country spent 4.1 nights away from home on average in 1989 and 3.6 nights in 1997; most tourists (70 %) now take short holidays (less than 4 nights). In France, the decrease in working hours, from 39 to 35 hours, has resulted in more days for holidays. There have been similar developments in several other European countries.

Tourism, and particularly mass tourism to some destinations, has become more attractive and easily accessible as a result of more packaged holidays being on offer, strong marketing strategies, low prices (particularly transport costs), the developing use of the internet for reservations, and the introduction of the euro currency in 12 EU countries. All this has led to more journeys per person and per year. As people become more affluent and the relative costs of travel and holidays fall, tourism is taking a larger and larger share of household expenditure on leisure.

In the EU, expenditure for recreation and culture increased by 60 % between 1990 and 2000, with EUR 435 billion spent in 2000, while the share of total expenditure increased from 9.2 % to 10.3 % over the same period. According to the Swiss Federal Statistical Office (2002), half of expenditure by Swiss citizens on transport, meals and beverages in 1998 was for leisure. The growth in tourism expenditure by households results mainly from the increase in transport, which accounts for the largest share of tourism expenditure.

Role of Environment

Transport

The most important regional environmental impact of tourism is from the associated transport. Travel to and from destinations is responsible for 90 % of the energy used in the tourism sector. In the EU, tourist travel represents 9 % of total passenger travel (including business travel, which constitutes 25-30 % of total passengerkm), and about 70 % of air transport is for holiday travel. For the whole EU, holiday transport is responsible for half of all passenger transport energy use, and 11 % of the overall energy consumption of the transport system (including freight).

In France, transport for domestic tourism contributes from 5 % to 7 % of all greenhouse gas emissions (IFEN, 2000). As tourism is growing more rapidly than overall traffic, the associated problems are likely to increase. The car offers a high degree of freedom for holidays and has also become cheaper relative to public transport than it was 20 years ago, giving it a special attractiveness for holiday travel (OECD, 2000). Some 340 million tourists arrived by road in southwestern Europe and EU accession countries in 1999. The modal shares of international tourist travel to southwestern European countries in 1997 were 61 % road, 30 % air, and only 4 % rail, putting especially high pressure on some areas.

For example, up to 80 % of all tourist journeys to the Alps, where public transport is crucially lacking, are by car. In the accession countries, 92 % of visitors come by road although the region has good access by train. Tourist travel is also highly concentrated in time, and the resulting seasonal saturation of road transport infrastructures often leads to decisions to supply more infrastructures and services. Although most air travel remains relatively short-distance, long-haul travel is the most rapidly growing form of tourist travel, both in absolute and percentage terms. There were 80 million arrivals by air in the southwestern and accession countries in 1999 (20 % of all arrivals), an increase of 60 % from 1990.

Of the 2 200 million day-trip journeys by UK tourists in 1998, the share of the train was less than 5 % (10 % for overnight trips) while that of the car remained above 80 %. Tourist trips in England made by UK residents increased by 60 % between 1990 and 1999, with air transport increasing by 213 %. Some subregions of the British rail network are already running at 90 % of capacity and most routes out of London will reach the same level by 2011 (English Tourism Council, 2001). There are similar developments in many countries and for all transport systems. Routes of strategic importance for tourism will need to be further considered if the transport system is to cope with the continuous growth of tourist flows expected during the next 10-20 years.

Travel patterns are changing: tourists are travelling more often, for shorter stays, and further from home, and the average roundtrip is getting longer than that for other purposes. In France, for example, the annual average distance travelled for tourism is 917 km per capita compared with 770 km for other purposes. The average person in the EU makes 0.8 tourist trips per year, travelling about 1 800 km; both these figures are likely to increase, with added impacts on the environment and on 'normal' traffic conditions.

Destinations

The direct local impacts of tourism on people and the environment at destinations are strongly affected by concentration in space and in time (seasonality). They result from the intensive use of water and land by the tourism and leisure facilities; the delivery and use of energy; changes in the landscape from the construction of infrastructure, buildings and facilities; air pollution and wastes; the compaction and sealing of soils (damage and destruction of vegetation); and the disturbance of fauna and local people (for example by noise). The growing number of tourists visiting sensitive natural areas, heightened by developments such as rural tourism around biosphere reserves, may jeopardize nature conservation. Some conflicts may also arise between tourism development and other sectors such as agriculture and forestry.

The uncontrolled development of tourism over recent decades has led to a dramatic degradation of the quality of the environment, especially around the Mediterranean and in the Alps. About 35 % of international tourist trips by Europeans are to the European Mediterranean countries (mostly to coastal areas) and 8 % to the Alps. Every year in the 1990s, it was estimated that nearly 135 million tourists (international and domestic) visited the Mediterranean coasts, doubling the local population. The impacts of the use of leisure boats and marinas are increasingly raising concerns in terms of pollution, over-use of natural sites and coastal zone management.

It is estimated that tourism contributes to 7 % of all pollution in the Mediterranean (industrial and urban wastes including sewage, polluted rivers draining into the sea, crude oil dumped by all activities, detergents, mercury, phosphates, eutrophication). Health problems such as infections of the ear, nose and throat, hepatitis, enteritis and dysentery can all result from swimming in some areas. Some destinations have become the victims of their own attractiveness. Islands such as Mykonos (Greece), Porquerolles and Ré (France), and Capri (Italy) that are experiencing increasing pressures have already exceeded their carrying capacity. The coastal strip (500 m from the shore) of Majorca, one of the most popular destinations, was already 27 % urbanised in 1995.

The over-use of water by hotels, swimming pools and golf courses is of particular concern in the Mediterranean and other regions where water is scarce. Tourists consume up to 300 litres (up to 880 litres for luxury tourism) and generate around 180 litres of wastewater per day. In the Balearic Islands, water consumption during the peak tourist month in 1999 (July) was equivalent to 20 % of that by the local population in a whole year, having increased by about 80 % since 1994. In the Rimini province (Italy), the production of wastes and wastewater in summer is three times higher than in winter, leading to some management problems.

The Alps are the second most favoured destination in Europe with 60 million arrivals per year, mainly because of the skiing facilities. Tourism is a key industry in many alpine areas, but it is also embedded in a wider socio-economic structure, with strong links with agriculture and other sectors. Tourism intensity can be considered as medium (0.1-0.5 tourist beds per local inhabitant) for 40 % of the Alpine communities and high (more than 0.5 beds per inhabitant) for approximately 20 %.

Tourism in mountain areas is responsible for changing the appearance of the landscape through buildings and facilities and disturbing fauna (for example by noise). The tracks of the heavy equipment that tend the ski slopes erode the thin topsoil on which the vegetation cover depends, and over-fertilization in summer causes severe losses of biodiversity. Tourism also results in water supply problems (including from the production of artificial snow, with snow blowers consuming 1m^3 of water for 2 m^3 of produced snow), and in sewage and waste disposal management difficulties. The waste generated in the isolated and high-altitude refuges is a crucial problem that may require special management such as transportation by helicopters.

The functioning of the ski lifts needs a great deal of energy (equivalent in the French Alps alone to one-third of the annual production of a nuclear power plant (IFEN, 2000). Accommodation (80 % of all tourism and leisure buildings) is a major source of impact, particularly on water resources, land use and ecosystems. Hotels are high consumers of water, as a tourist staying in a hotel uses on average one third more water per day than a local inhabitant. Energy consumption per m2 per year by a one star hotel is 157 kWh (380 kWh in a four star hotel). Some tourism businesses are starting to implement energy-efficiency measures, for example hotels in the United Kingdom 'saved' up to 9 000 tonnes of carbon dioxide per year each between 1997 and 1999.

Campsites are supposed to be a reversible form of land use, but water supply, sewage and waste disposal problems can arise if the infrastructure is not designed to cope with peak periods. The growth in the number of second homes during the 1990s constitutes another major problem. The land area required by such a home, estimated at around 100 m2 per person, represents 40 times that for a flat rental and 160 times that for an 80-bed hotel in a year (20 times that for an 80-bed hotel when garden areas are excluded). Most construction is in coastal zones and skiing areas. In Sweden, about one third of second homes are 100 m from the shore.

In France, the world's top tourist destination, almost 335 000 new second homes have been built during the past two decades, covering more than 22 million m2 of land; second homes now represent 73 % of total tourist lodging capacity, and 18 % of all nights spent by residents in 1999 were in their second home. Moreover, most second homes are seldom used: often only two weeks a year compared to more than 20 weeks for hotels. In Portugal, some families travel every summer weekend to a second home, at a considerable distance. The continuing demand for high quality, luxurious and comfortable accommodation is expected to result in a steady growth in the number of holidays spent in hotels and second homes.

Management Policies

Progress in addressing the sustainable development of tourism is mainly at the destination level, generally with a regulatory approach in the southwestern European countries and a more market-based approach in the northwestern countries, through voluntary agreements and eco-labelling schemes. At the regional level, tourism is covered in the Mediterranean area by the Barcelona convention and the Mediterranean action plan, in the Alps by the additional protocol on tourism to the Alpine convention, and in the Baltic by Agenda 21 for the Baltic Sea region.

Most policy developments at the local level are through Local Agenda 21, with up to 35 % of European municipalities committed to plans that stress tourism as a priority. Vital public/private sector collaborative links are being developed at a number of leading destinations. For instance, and as a transnational experiment, 13 natural parks in six western European countries have committed to the criteria of the 'Charter on sustainable tourism in natural protected areas' that is supported by the Europarc Federation. Hoteliers and other tourism businesses could play a significant role in the development of sustainable tourism and benefit directly from environmental initiatives, but very few have adopted environmental management systems.

Eco-labelling has shown some potential but its use, while growing, remains small. Recent surveys suggest that many people would pay extra for accommodation that was part of a green accreditation scheme. The external costs that tourism imposes on the local and regional environment and population are complex and depend on the characteristics of tourism in each type of destination. The impacts on society as a whole are associated with transport systems. Economic instruments such as environmental taxes are used in some countries, with visitors paying direct and indirect taxes on tourism products and services, but the revenues are not generally directed to environmental protection or improvement.

At the same time, some popular destinations receive special subventions from the state for tourism infrastructures. In 1995, the European Council in its Recommendation R(95)10, relating to a policy for the development of sustainable tourism in natural protected areas, recommended allocating part of the tax on overnight stays to financing environmental infrastructures and the preservation of the environment. In Austria, the Land of Salzburg instituted in 1992 a tax on second homes that is allocated to local actions for preserving the landscape. The Balearic Islands levy an ecotax on hotel stays and a tax on passenger transport to small islands is levied in France. A diving tax (EUR 2.30 per dive) in the natural reserve in Medes Islands (Catalonia, Spain) generated EUR 130 000 in 1996, i.e. 68 % of the budget of the reserve.

Different European countries have different institutional frameworks for tourism, from regional boards to state ministries, and some programmes that are designed to encourage sustainable tourism are being developed. However, most of the environmental measures that have so far been implemented have been initiated by major tour operators and local stakeholders and are based on voluntary approaches. There is a general lack of broad environmentally integrated strategies for the sector.

Economics Impacts

Tourism's economic impacts are therefore an important consideration in state, regional and community planning and economic development. Economic impacts are also important factors in marketing and management decisions. Communities therefore need to understand the relative importance of tourism to their region, including tourism's contribution to economic activity in the area. A variety of methods, ranging from pure guesswork to complex mathematical models, are used to estimate tourism's economic impacts.

Different kinds of economic analysis are frequently confused, let's begin by positioning economic impact studies within the broader set of economic problems and techniques relevant to tourism. These same techniques may be applied to any policy or action, but we will define them here in the context of tourism. Each type of analysis is identified by the basic question(s) it answers and the types of methods and models that are appropriate. Benefit cost analysis and economic impact analysis are frequently confused as both discuss economic "benefits". There are two clear distinctions between the two techniques. B/C analysis addresses the benefits from economic efficiency while economic impact analysis focuses on the regional distribution of economic activity.

The income received from tourism by a destination region is largely off-set by corresponding losses in the origin regions, yielding only modest contributions to net social welfare and efficiency. B/C analysis includes both market and non-market values (consumer surplus), while economic impact analysis is restricted to actual flows of money from market transactions. While each type of economic analysis is somewhat distinct, a given problem often calls for several different kinds of economic analysis. An economic impact study will frequently involve a demand analysis to project levels of tourism activity.

In other cases demand is treated as exogenous and the analysis simply estimates impacts if a given number of visitors are attracted to the area. A comprehensive impact assessment will also examine fiscal impacts, as well as social and environmental impacts. Be aware that an economic impact analysis, by itself, provides a rather narrow and often one-sided perspective on the impacts of tourism. Studies of the economic impacts of tourism tend to emphasize the positive benefits of tourism.

On the other hand environmental, social, cultural and fiscal impact studies tend to focus more on negative impacts of tourism. This is in spite of the fact that there are negative economic impacts of tourism (e.g., seasonality and lower wage jobs) and in many cases positive environmental and social impacts (e.g., protection of natural & cultural resources in the area and education of both tourists and local residents). An economic impact assessment (EIA) traces changes in economic activity resulting from some action. An EIA will identify which economic sectors benefit from tourism and estimate resulting changes in income and employment in the region.

Economic impact assessment procedures do not assess economic efficiency and also do not generally produce estimates of the fiscal costs of an action. For many problems economic impact analysis will be part of a broader analysis.

Environmental, social, and fiscal impacts are often equally important concerns in a balanced assessment of impacts.

An economic impact analysis will assess the contribution of tourism activity to a region's economy. It also reveals the interrelationships among economic sectors and provides estimates of the changes that take place in an economy due to some existing or proposed action. The most common applications of economic impact analysis to tourism are:

— To evaluate the economic impacts of changes in the supply of recreation and tourism opportunities. Supply changes may involve a change in quantity, such as the opening of new facilities, closing of existing ones, or expansions and contraction in capacity. Supply changes may also involve changes in quality, including changes in

  a) the quality of the environment,

  b) the local infrastructure and public services to support tourism, or

  c) the nature of the tourism products and services that are provided in an area.

— To evaluate the economic impacts of changes in tourism demand. Population changes, changes in the competitive position of the region, marketing activity or changing consumer tastes and preferences can alter levels of tourism activity, spending, and associated economic activity. An economic impact study can estimate the magnitude and nature of these impacts.

— To evaluate the effects of policies and actions which affect tourism activity either directly or indirectly. Tourism depends on many factors at both origins and destinations that are frequently outside the direct control of the tourism industry itself. Economic impact studies provide information to help decision makers better understand the consequences of various actions on the tourism industry as well as on other sectors of the economy. For example, increased air pollution standards have been opposed in some regions due to the predicted economic consequences of the closing of plants that cannot meet the new standards. Tourism interests counter these arguments with estimates of the potential gains in income and jobs in tourism industries that depend on good air quality and visibility.

— To understand the economic structure and interdependencies of different sectors of the economy. Economic studies help us better understand the size and structure of the tourism industry in a given region and its linkages to other sectors of the economy. Such understandings are helpful in identifying potential partners for the tourism industry as well as in targeting industries as part of regional economic development strategies. Issues such as economic growth, stability, and seasonality may be addressed as part of these studies.

— To argue for favorable treatment in allocation of resources or local tax, zoning or other policy decisions. By showing that tourism has significant economic impacts, tourism interests can often convince decision-makers to allocate more resources for tourism or to establish policies that encourage tourism. Tax abatements and other incentives frequently given to manufacturing firms have also been granted to hotels, marinas and other tourism businesses based on demonstrated economic impacts in the local area.

— To compare the economic impacts of alternative resource allocation, policy, management or development proposals. Economic impact analyses are commonly used to assess the relative merits of distinct alternatives. The economic contribution of expanded tourism offerings may be compared for example with alternatives such as resource extraction activities (mining, timber harvesting) or manufacturing. Impacts of alternative tourism development proposals may also be evaluated, e.g., tourism strategies that emphasize outdoor recreation, camping development, a convention facility, or a factory outlet mall.

Tourism has a variety of economic impacts. Tourists contribute to sales, profits, jobs, tax revenues, and income in an area. The most direct effects occur within the primary tourism sectors-lodging, restaurants, transportation, amusements, and retail trade . Through secondary effects, tourism affects most sectors of the economy. An economic impact analysis of tourism activity normally focuses on changes in sales, income, and employment in a region resulting from tourism activity.

A simple tourism impact scenario illustrates. Let's say a region attracts an additional 100 tourists, each spending $100 per day. That's $10,000 in new spending per day in the area. If sustained over a 100 day season, the region would accumulate a million dollars in new sales. The million dollars in spending would be distributed to lodging, restaurant, amusement and retail trade sectors in proportion to how the visitor spends the $100. Perhaps 30% of the million dollars would leak out of the region immediately to cover the costs of goods purchased by tourists that are not made in the local area (only the retail margins for such items should normally be included as direct sales effects).

The remaining $700,000 in direct sales might yield $350,000 in income within tourism industries and support 20 direct tourism jobs. Tourism industries are labor and income intensive, translating a high proportion of sales into income and corresponding jobs. The tourism industry, in turn, buys goods and services from other businesses in the area, and pays out most of the $350,000 in income as wages and salaries to its employees. This creates secondary economic effects in the region. The study might use a sales multiplier of 2.0 to indicate that each dollar of direct sales generates another dollar in secondary sales in this region.

Through multiplier effects, the $700,000 in direct sales produces $1.4 million in total sales. These secondary sales create additional income and employment, resulting in a total impact on the region of $1.4 million in sales, $650,000 in income and 35 jobs. While hypothetical, the numbers used here are fairly typical of what one might find in a tourism economic impact study. A more complete study might identify which sectors receive the direct and secondary effects and possibly identify differences in spending and impacts of distinct subgroups of tourists (market segments). One can also estimate the tax effects of this spending by applying local tax rates to the appropriate changes in sales or income.

Instead of focusing on visitor spending, one could also estimate impacts of construction or government activity associated with tourism. There are several other categories of economic impacts that are not typically covered in economic impact assessments, at least not directly. For example:

— Changes in prices-tourism can sometimes inflate the cost of housing and retail prices in the area, frequently on a seasonal basis.

— Changes in the quality and quantity of goods and services - tourism may lead to a wider array of goods and services available in an area (of either higher or lower quality than without tourism).

— Changes in property and other taxes - taxes to cover the cost of local services may be higher or lower in the presence of tourism activity. In some cases, taxes collected directly or indirectly from tourists may yield reduced local taxes for schools, roads, etc. In other cases, locals may be taxed more heavily to cover the added infrastructure and service costs. The impacts of tourism on local government costs and revenues are addressed more fully in a fiscal impact analysis.

— Economic dimensions of "social" and "environmental" impacts - There are also economic consequences of most social and environmental impacts that are not usually addressed in an economic impact analysis. These can be positive or negative. For example, traffic congestion will increase costs of moving around for both households and businesses. Improved amenities that attract tourists may also encourage retirees or other kinds of businesses to locate in the area.

Direct, Indirect and Induced Effects

A standard economic impact analysis traces flows of money from tourism spending, first to businesses and government agencies where tourists spend their money and then to :

— other businesses-supplying goods and services to tourist businesses,

— households - earning income by working in tourism or supporting industries, and

— government-through various taxes and charges on tourists, businesses and households

Indirect and induced effects are sometimes collectively called secondary effects. The total economic impact of tourism is the sum of direct, indirect, and induced effects within a region. Any of these impacts may be measured as gross output or sales, income, employment, or value added. Direct effects are production changes associated with the immediate effects of changes in tourism expenditures. For example, an increase in the number of tourists staying overnight in hotels would directly yield increased sales in the hotel sector.

The additional hotel sales and associated changes in hotel payments for wages and salaries, taxes, and supplies and services are direct effects of the tourist spending. Indirect effects are the production changes resulting from various rounds of re-spending of the hotel industry's receipts in other backward-linked industries (i.e., industries supplying products and services to hotels). Changes in sales, jobs, and income in the linen supply industry, for example, represent indirect effects of changes in hotel sales. Businesses supplying products and services to the linen supply industry represent another round of indirect effects, eventually linking hotels to varying degrees to many other economic sectors in the region.

Induced effects are the changes in economic activity resulting from household spending of income earned directly or indirectly as a result of tourism spending. For example, hotel and linen supply employees, supported directly or indirectly by tourism, spend their income in the local region for housing, food, transportation, and the usual array of household product and service needs. The sales, income, and jobs that result from household spending of added wage, salary, or proprietor's income are induced effects.

By means of indirect and induced effects, changes in tourist spending can impact virtually every sector of the economy in one way or another. The magnitude of secondary effects depends on the propensity of businesses and households in the region to purchase goods and services from local suppliers. Induced effects are particularly noticed when a large employer in a region closes a plant. Not only are supporting industries (indirect effects) hurt, but the entire local economy suffers due to the reduction in household income within the region. Retail stores close and leakages of money from the region increase as consumers go outside the region for more and more goods and services.

Final demand is the term used by economists for sales to the final consumers of goods and services. In almost all cases, the final consumers of tourism goods and services are households. Government spending is also considered as final demand. The same methods for estimating impacts of visitor spending can be applied to estimate the economic impacts of government spending, for example, to operate and maintain a park or visitor center.

Regional Economic Models

An input-output model (I-O model) is a mathematical model that describes the flows of money between sectors within a region's economy. Flows are predicted by knowing what each industry must buy from every other industry to produce a dollar's worth of output. Using each industry's production function, I-O models also determine the proportions of sales that go to wage and salary income, proprietor's income, and taxes. Multipliers can be estimated from input-output models based on the estimated re-circulation of spending within the region.

Exports and imports are determined based upon estimates of the propensity of households and firms within the region to purchase goods and services from local sources (often called RPC's or regional purchase coefficients). The more a region is self-sufficient and purchases goods and services from within the region, the higher the multipliers for the region. Input-output models make a number of assumptions. The basic ones are that:

— All firms in a given industry employ the same production technology (usually assumed to be the national average for that industry), and produce identical products.

— There are no economies or diseconomies of scale in production or factor substitution. I-O models are essentially linear-double the level of tourism activity/ production and you double all of the inputs, the number of jobs, etc.

- The model doesn't explicitly keep track of time, but analysts generally report the impact estimates as if they represent activity within a single year.
- One must assume that the various model parameters are accurate and represent the current year. I-O models are firmly grounded in the national system of accounts, which relies on a standard industrial classification system (SIC codes) and various federal government economic censuses, in which individual firms report sales, wage and salary payments and employment. I-O models will generally be at least a few years out-of-date, although this isn't usually a major problem unless the region's economy has changed significantly. An I-O model represents the region's economy at a particular point in time. Tourist spending estimates are generally price adjusted to the year of the model.
- Multiplier computations for induced effects generally assume that jobs created by additional spending are new jobs, involving new households in the area. Induced effects are computed assuming linear changes in household spending with changes in income. Estimates of induced effects may be inflated due to the violation of these assumptions. Induced effects tend to account for the vast majority of the secondary effects of tourism, and therefore should be used with caution.

Multipliers Effects

Multipliers capture the secondary economic effects (indirect and induced) of tourism activity. Multipliers have been frequently misused and misinterpreted in tourism studies and are a considerable source of confusion among non-economists. Multipliers represent the economic interdependencies between sectors within a particular region's economy. They vary considerably from region to region and sector to sector. There are many different kinds of multipliers reflecting which secondary effects are included and which measure of economic activity is used (sales, income, or employment).

The multipliers are called ratio type multipliers as they measure the ratio of a total impact measure to the corresponding direct impact. Comparable income and employment ratio type multipliers may be defined by replacing sales with measures of income or employment Ratio multipliers should be used with caution. A common error is to multiply a sales multiplier times tourist spending to get total sales effects. This will generate an inflated estimate of tourism impacts. The problem is that tourism spending or sales is not exactly the same as the "direct effects", appearing in the multiplier formula.

Tourist purchases of goods are the primary source of the problem. To properly apply tourist purchases of goods to an input-output model (or corresponding multipliers), various margins (retail, wholesale and transportation) must be deducted from the "purchaser price" of the good to separate out the "producer price". In an I-O model, retail margins accrue to the retail trade sector, wholesale margins to wholesale trade, transportation margins to transportation sectors (trucking, rail, air etc.) and the producer prices of goods are assigned to the sector that produces the good.

In most cases the factory that produces the good bought by a tourist lies outside of the local region, creating an immediate "leakage" in the first round of spending and therefore no local impact from production of the good. Before applying a multiplier to tourist spending, one must first deduct the producer prices of all imported goods that tourists buy (i.e. only include the local retail margins and possibly wholesale and transportation margins if these firms lie within the region). Generally, only 60 to 70% of tourist spending appears as final demand in a local region.

While all tourist purchases of services will accrue to the local region as final demand , only the margins on goods purchased at retail stores should be counted as local final demand. The ratio of local final demand to tourist spending is called the capture rate. Capture rate = local final demand / tourism spending in local area. The distinction between Type II and Type III multipliers involves a technical difference in how the induced effects are computed. Type II approaches include households as a sector of the economy and invert the technical coefficient matrix including the household sector, while Type III approaches treat households as exogenous.

Capture rates, like multipliers, will vary with the size and nature of the region as well as the kind of tourist spending included. One must therefore be cautious in taking a multiplier or capture rate cited in one study and using it in another.

Another way of calculating a multiplier (generally the preferred approach among economists) is as a ratio of income or employment to sales. This kind of multiplier is sometimes called a Keynesian multiplier or response coefficient. Type III Income multiplier = Total direct, indirect, and induced income direct sales Type III Employment multiplier = Total direct, indirect, and induced employment direct sales This income (employment) multiplier produces total income (employment) impacts when multiplied by the direct sales. One must still be careful in distinguishing between tourism spending/sales and direct sales effects. Some studies may embed the capture rate in the multiplier, expressing the ratio in terms of tourism spending rather than direct sales.

Measurement of Tourism

The economic impacts of tourism are typically estimated by some variation of the following simple formula: Economic Impact of Tourism = Number of Tourists * Average Spending per Visitor * Multiplier. The formula suggests three distinct steps and corresponding measurements or models:

Estimate the change in the number and types of tourists to the region due to the proposed policy or action.

Estimates or projections of tourist activity generally come from a demand model or some system for measuring levels of tourism activity in an area. Economic impact estimates will rest heavily on good estimates of the numbers and types of visitors. These must come from carefully designed measurements of tourist activity, a good demand model, or good judgement. This step is usually the weakest link in most tourism impact studies, as few regions have accurate counts of tourists, let alone good models for predicting changes in tourism activity or separating local visitors from visitors from outside the region.

Estimate average levels of spending (often within specific market segments) of tourists in the local area.

Spending averages come from sample surveys or are sometimes borrowed or adapted from other studies. Spending estimates must be based on a representative sample of the population of tourists taking into account variations across seasons, types of tourists, and locations within the study area. As spending can vary widely across different kinds of tourists, we recommend estimating average spending for a set of key tourist segments based on samples of at least 50-100 visitors within each tourism segment. Segments should be defined to capture differences in spending between local residents vs. tourists, day users vs. overnight visitors, type of accommodation, and type of transportation.

In broadly based tourism impact studies, it is useful to identify unique spending patterns of important activity segments such as downhill skiers, boaters, convention & business travelers. Multiplying the number of tourists by the average spending per visitor (be careful the units are consistent) gives an estimate of total tourist spending in the area. Estimates of tourist spending will generally be more accurate if distinct spending profiles and use estimates are made for key tourism segments. The use and spending estimates are the two most important parts of an economic impact assessment. When combined, they capture the amount of money brought into the region by tourists. Multipliers are needed only if one is interested in the secondary effects of tourism spending.

Apply the change in spending to a regional economic model or set of multipliers to determine secondary effects.

Secondary effects of tourism are estimated using multipliers or a model of the region's economy. Multipliers generally come from an economic base or input-output model of the region's economy. In many cases multipliers are borrowed (often improperly) or adjusted from published multipliers or other studies. One should not take a multiplier estimated for one region and apply it in a region with a quite different economic structure. Generally, multipliers are higher for larger regions with more diversified economies and lower for smaller regions with more limited economic development. A common error is to apply a statewide multiplier (since these are more widely published) to a local region. This will yield inflated estimates of local multiplier effects.

Multipliers can also be used to convert estimates of spending or sales to income and employment. Simple ratios can be used to capture how much income or jobs are generated per dollar of sales. These ratios will vary from region to region and across individual economic sectors due to the relative importance of labor inputs in each industry and different wage and salary rates in different regions of the country. Be aware that job estimates are generally not full time equivalents, making them difficult to compare across industries with different proportions of seasonal and part time jobs. Income or value addedare generally the preferred measures of the contribution of tourism to a region's economy.

Approaches of Economic Impact

Different levels of detail and corresponding expense (time and money) and accuracy are possible for each of the three steps-estimating tourist volume, spending, and multiplier effects. Four typical approaches illustrate the levels of detail that are possible and the associated methods.

— Subjective estimates that rely mostly on expert opinion
— Secondary data in aggregate form, adapting existing estimates to suit the problem
— Secondary data in disaggregate form, permitting finer adjustment of data to fit the situation
— Primary data and/or formal models, usually involving visitor surveys and regional economic models.

One can employ different levels of aggregation in visitor segments, spending categories, multipliers, and economic sectors to finely tune the data and models to a particular application and also yield more detailed information about the economic impacts. For example, spending data from previous surveys may be adjusted over time using consumer price indices (CPI). If spending is itemized in several categories, distinct CPI's may be used for food away from home, lodging, or gasoline. If not, an aggregate CPI, which may not reflect the mix of goods that tourists purchase, must be used.

Data for distinct tourism market segments is also valuable in tailoring secondary data to a particular application. For example, separate estimates of the average spending for day users and overnight visitors allows one to adjust the spending estimate to reflect a given mix of day users and overnight visitors.

The WTTC effort also focuses on national and statewide accounting of tourism's economic significance.

Their satellite tourism account identifies the contribution of travel and tourism to gross national product (GNP) or gross state product (GSP). Using the standard national system of accounts, they identify the portion of sales, taxes and investment attributable directly to travel and tourism. The WTTC system does not use multipliers or attempt to estimate secondary effects. It does, however, capture a great deal of travel-related economic activity, not covered by visitor trip spending, such as durable goods purchases (boats and RV's), construction and investment in tourism, and government expenditures.

Bibliography

Brotherton, B. (ed.) *The Handbook of Contemporary Hospitality Management Research* Chichester: Wiley, 1999.

Clark, M. *Interpersonal Skills for Hospitality Management* London: Chapman & Hall, 1995.

Cullen, P. *Economics for Hospitality Management* London: International Thomson Business Press, 1997.

Davis, B. and Stone, S. *Food and Beverage Management* Oxford: Butterworth-Heinemann, 1998.

Horner, S. *Marketing Tourism, Hospitality and Leisure in Europe* London: International Thomson Business Press, 1996.

Johns, N. et al *Operational Techniques: a resource-based approach for the hospitality industry* London: Cassell, 1994.

Jones, P. (ed.) *Introduction to Hospitality Operations* London: Cassell, 1996.

__________ . and Pizam, A. (eds.) *The International Hospitality Industry: organizational and operational issues* Harlow: Longman, 1995.

Knowles, T. *Corporate Strategy for Hospitality* Harlow: Longman, 1996.

Lockwood, A. et al (eds.) *Quality Management in Hospitality: best practice in action* London: Cassell, 1996.

Mullins, L. J. *Managing People in the Hospitality Industry* Harlow: Longman, 1998.

Powers, T. F. *Introduction to the Hospitality Industry* New York: Wiley, 1999 (4th edition) ISBN: 0471252441

Riley, M. *Human Resources Management in the Hospitality and Tourism Industry* Oxford: Butterworth-Heinemann, 1996.

Sargent, M. and Lyle, T. *Successful Pubs and Inns* Oxford: Butterworth-Heinemann, 1998.

Taylor, D. *Hospitality Sales and Promotion: strategies for success* Oxford: Butterworth-Heinemann, 2001

Teare, R., Bowen, J. T. and Hing, N. (eds.) *New Directions in Hospitality and Tourism: a worldwide review* London: Cassell, 1998

Wood, R. C. and Verginis, C. S. (eds.) *Accommodation Management: perspectives for the international hotel industry* London: International Thomson Business Press, 1999

Index